CW00456966

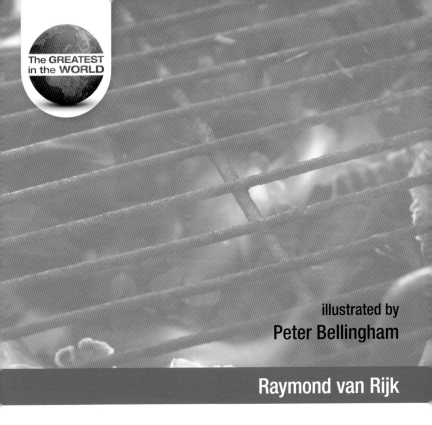

illustrated by
Peter Bellingham

Raymond van Rijk

The Greatest

Barbeque

Tips in the World

A 'The Greatest in the World' Book

www.thegreatestintheworld.com

Illustrations:
Peter Bellingham
www.peterbellinghamillustration.co.uk

Cover & layout design:
The designcouch
www.designcouch.co.uk

Cover images: © Paul Cowan; © Paula Gent; © Lee March;
© David Smith courtesy of www.fotolia.com

Copy editor.
Bronwyn Robertson
www.theartsva.com

Series creator/editor:
Steve Brookes

First edition published in 2006 by Public Eye Publications

Thi edition published in 2007 by
The Greatest in the World Ltd, PO Box 3182,
Stratford-upon-Avon, Warwickshire CV37 7XW

Text and Illustrations Copyright © 2007 – The Greatest in the World Ltd.

A CIP catalogue record for this book is available from the British Library
ISBN 978-1-905151-68-4

Printed and bound in China by 1010 Printing International Ltd.

I would like to dedicate this book to two people who inspired me with food, my mother Anna and my friend chef Noel Crawford, and to my wife Kirsty for her support, encouragement and, mostly, patience.

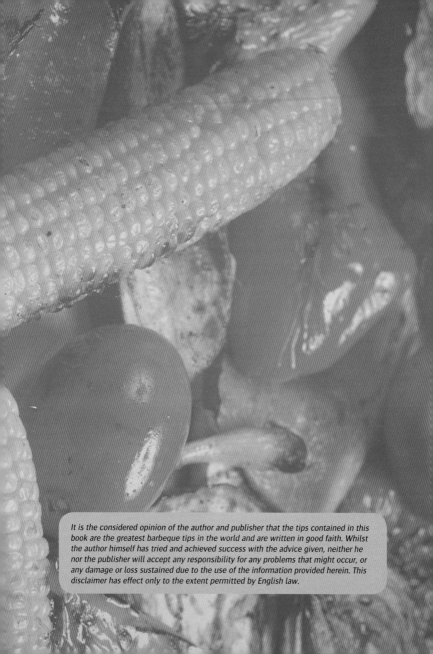

Contents

A few words from Raymond …

I started teaching barbequing when I noticed that everywhere I went there were really good quality barbecues sitting on the terrace, but they were only employed to grill a few chops and sausages. Many people lacked the confidence and technique to cook on a barbeque, and I decided to turn that around. Once I began teaching barbequing, I realised how many people there were who really wanted to get barbequing, but had been held back by the public nature of this kind of cooking. Who wants to cook by trial and error with an audience?

Of course barbequing is the perfect way to combine both social life and feasting, and I think this is much of the attraction for most people. But if you feel afraid to get out and do it because you don't know how, I sincerely hope this book will give you the good sound advice that will revive the pleasure and flavour of barbequing for you, and get you out of the kitchen and back to where the party is really happening. I have barbequed and spit roasted for more than twenty five years, yet I never become bored with this very particular style of cookery. The world offers a vast array of versions of barbequing, from Japanese Hibachi to American Pit Barbeque. I hope this book will bring a little of this exotic breadth to your dinner table.

I'm delighted to have had the chance to produce this book for The Greatest in the World team. It is an excellent opportunity to get really practical useful information into the hands of barbequers of all skill levels and it is intended to give you the really important information that recipes don't include! Whilst this is not a cookbook, it does include some of my favourite recipes. While I can lay claim to devising quite a few of them, some are from the many gifted amateurs and professional barbeque chefs I have met over the years.

Once you understand the techniques, the ingredients and the ways you can flavour food, you will be able to use any recipe, and then begin to devise your own. I sincerely hope this book will open the door to new ways of preparing food, introducing flavour and arm you with the skills to be confident in your barbequing.

May your barbeques—whenever or wherever you have them —be the best ever!

Happy grilling!

Grilling, broiling, barbecuing – whatever you want to call it – is an art, not just a matter of building a pyre and throwing on a piece of meat as a sacrifice to the gods of the stomach.

James Beard, Beard on Food *(1974)*

Barbequing & grilling

chapter 1
Barbequing and grilling

Getting hot hot hot!

Temperature control is the most important aspect, and biggest challenge, to the barbequer. When it comes to temperature control and cooking on wood or charcoal, the old saying that 'nothing beats experience' holds true. The more you do, the better you will be at understanding and controlling the barbeque temperature. So practise, practise, practise.

Heat control on raw fuel fires is gained in three ways: by adjustments to the height of the grill over the heat source, opening or closing the vents on the barbeque, or adding to or reducing the quantity of fuel. The first most obvious technique is the amount and distribution of fuel. Add more for more heat. Spreading the charcoal unevenly will give some areas of hotter or cooler cooking. Opening or closing the vents add or reduce oxygen, which will heat up that fire, or damp it down.

Low, medium or hot?

How hot is 'medium'? One man's medium could be another's hot. Most recipes and cooking advice will understand low, medium or hot to be within the range of the following listed temperatures. Cooking temperatures for grilling can vary from 150°C/300°F (low) to 180°C/350°F (medium) to 250°C/480°F (high).

In the barbeque is any four footed animal – be it mouse or mastodon – whose dressed carcass is roasted whole … at its best it is a fat steer, and must be eaten within an hour of when it is cooked. For if ever the sun rises upon a barbeque, its flavour vanishes like Cinderella's silks, and it becomes cold beef – staler in the chill dawn then illicit love.

William Allen White (1864–1944)

Direct, or indirect, that is the question

There's grilling and there's grilling. That is to say, direct grilling and indirect grilling. Confused? Wait, there's more: different ingredients require different cooking techniques. Worried? Don't be. It's all quite simple.

Direct grilling is placing the food directly over the heat source (see, I told you it was simple). Indirect grilling is having the heat supplied from beside (but not directly under) the food. The heat is reflected, so indirect is used in hooded or lidded barbeques. Indirect is placing food beside the heat source.

DIRECT GRILLING
Direct grilling (cooking directly over the heat source) is best suited to items that are relatively small, such as a steak, fillet of fish, burger, satay, sausage, mushroom, etc., and needs a short grilling time of about 3–15 minutes, and cooking temperatures are 200°C/400°F and higher.

Indirect approach for big cuts

Large food items, such as a whole chicken, whole eye or scotch fillets, a leg of lamb or whole fish, should be cooked using the indirect grill method. Ensure the food is NOT over the heat source, move charcoal or briquettes to the sides of the barbeque, or if using gas, turn central gas jets off. Cover with hood or lid. Cooking times for this method could vary from 15 minutes for a side of salmon to 4 hours for a shoulder of pork.

Tool + fuel = heat control

The secret of good barbequing is temperature control. Once you have that, then the size and type of foods, the style of cookery and the speed will follow.

Heat control is achieved with the tool (i.e. the type of barbeque you use) and the fuel.

As you barbeque more you will become more skilful, understand the idiosyncrasies of your particular barbeque—and yourself—and what once seemed so difficult will become second nature. Read the manual that comes with your model of barbeque, pay special attention to information about heat control, and notice how the barbeque reacts to different weather conditions.

Start me up

It's the most obvious thing we often forget. I've embarrassed myself by fiddling with switches and gas bottles, and getting nowhere, only to realise the gas bottle is empty, or the knob is turned off. First turn all knobs to OFF position, then check gas bottle is full, properly connected and ready. Open the hood, make sure the barbeque is clean and the drip tray is empty. Turn the gas valve on. Light the grill according to the instructions for that model. Most have starter buttons. If not, long handled matches or a gas lighter are advisable. DO NOT put your hand inside the gas jet area.

Buying a barbeque

chapter 2
Buying a barbeque

Plate or grill?

I admit I'm not a big fan of the plate. Barbequing on a plate will not give the food that special barbeque flavour, and the fuel you choose is largely irrelevant, as it will not add to the flavour of the food. This is because the juices of the meats remain on the plate when meats start to cook. When you cook on a grill, flavour that is created when the meat juices evaporate on the charcoal, briquettes, flame tamers or gas elements, impart an aromatic and smoky flavour to the food above. A thicker plate will retain heat even if the intensity of the wood fire starts to vary. A slightly thinner plate can be used if a constant high heat source (gas or electricity) is used. The temperature of thin plates is more easily adjusted.

Electric barbeque.
Sound like an oxymoron to you?

It does to me. I can't see the sense in moving your stove outdoors. Why not just cook in the kitchen? The same way thermal underwear is a passion killer, an electric barbeque destroys the thrill and adventure of the outdoor meal – not to mention your chance to really prove your worth. Excuse me if my prejudice is showing, but you won't see me using one of these. Of course it is easier and safer than charcoal and gas and you won't easily run out of electricity.

A barrel of laughs!

The Horizontal Barrel Smoker is more common in North America than Europe and down under. It has a cylindrical smoke chamber, a firebox and a chimney. The chimney can be large enough to accommodate food for smoking; the chamber can be large enough to cook for a substantial number of hungry guests. Whole logs commonly fuel it, but briquettes and charcoal are also used. Soaked wood chunks create more smoke to flavour food. If you have plenty of time, and like a good strong smoked flavour in your food, this is the ideal barbeque for you.

Charcoal barbeques

The range of styles (and prices) of charcoal barbeques is huge. The most simple and inexpensive are disposable charcoal barbeques. These have a number of drawbacks – they lack adjustable vents, hoods and height adjustable grills. But they are easy to use and no clean up is necessary as you just throw them away. From the simplicity of a tinfoil box the range extends to highly sophisticated bigger capacity style kettle barbeques (that look like the alien invasion has begun in your back yard), and a whole lot in between. If you plan to make regular use of the barbeque, then look further up the range.

For charcoal barbequing you should look for adjustable vents to control airflow, variable positioning of the grill to allow you to alter the heat your food is subjected to, a rotisserie, and a hood to make indirect grilling possible. Once you've decided what capacity you require – do you want to indirect grill a whole animal? A large fish? A turkey? – Then it is time to go shopping.

Permanent grill barbeque

A brick or stone barbeque built in your backyard can be a great asset and looks great if it can be made to blend with the look of the house. When designing it remember to allow for an adjustable grill rack, then you can easily lower or raise your food over the heat source, thus altering the heat on the food. Charcoal, briquettes or wood can be used. Some outdoor kitchen units can be built into a brick or stone garden structure. These are usually gas fuelled. With either type, plan the location of fuel in the design (gas bottle out of sight? convenient wood storage?) and also an area for food, food preparation and utensils. (Where will you put food? Where will your utensils and ingredients sit?). Plan for weather conditions too, build the barbeque so it is sheltered with lots of bench space!

Gas barbeque

Gas barbeques come in all shapes and sizes. I have worked with tabletop versions of the kettle, and monsters that look as if only a crew of military personnel should be handling them. The gas barbeques on the market today include many sophisticated new fangled adaptations and additions. While some of these might appear unnecessary, the changes made to models are often improvements in both efficiency and style.

Barbequing has advanced a long way from the charring of meat on an open fire, and this is why what used to be called barbeques are now referred to, in the upper market range, as "outdoor kitchens". These are designed to offer barbeque style food but with the ease and convenience of the indoor kitchen. They also allow for a longer barbeque season.

Heat and gas

Adjusting the heat on gas barbeques is easy, just turn the knob. Most come with a thermometer in the hood, so you can easily see that you have the heat you want. However, different makes of barbeque can produce different ranges of temperature. I've worked on some that just couldn't get the high temperatures I needed, no matter how far the knob was turned or how fiercely the burners hissed. Some won't allow for cooler temperatures.

To find the best BBQ you can use trial and error, but better yet, ask the sales representative about the product. Have they used it themselves? Ask your friends and watch them while they cook, help a mate while he barbeques. Read the information, of course they are trying to sell you something, but a good quality barbeque should have estimated temperature ranges listed in the product brochure. Go to their website and look for the information or email them with a specific question if you can't find out any other way. It isn't any fun trying to cook a great steak on a slow low heat barbeque; you need to know before you buy.

What to look for in a gas BBQ

Gas barbeques are ideal if you are interested in developing your barbeque skills, you like to entertain at home, you have both time and space, and you grill year round.

What to look for:

- Heat output and grill system.

- The elements – stainless steel or cast iron. Cast iron tends to rust.

- Heat output. This is usually expressed in BTUs (British thermal units), kilowatts or megajoules. The higher the BTU the hotter the grill, but hotter is not always necessarily better. Americans and Canadians grill more with hood and lower heats. Australians, New Zealanders and the British tend to prefer hoodless and higher heats. Higher heat output could cause problems with grilling if the ventilation in the hooded barbeque is not properly designed. Well designed barbeques retain the heat.

- Number of elements – I recommend more than one element, allowing better heat control, and different heat zones on the grill.

- Above the elements there is usually a system to catch and evaporate the cooking juices while grilling. These vapours give the food that typical BBQ flavour. The systems are flame tamers and could be a cast iron unit, lava rocks, ceramic rocks or flavour bars (designed by Weber). These prevent fat and juices from blocking the gas jets and avoid flare ups.

- The grilling is done on grills or plates, which can be cast iron, stainless steel, or porcelain coated aluminium.

- Some barbeques have a side burner, handy to prepare sauces, stir-fry vegetables, or potatoes.

- Knobs should not be flimsy and the barbeque should have an igniter.

Questions to consider

When looking for a barbeque ask yourself ...

- Do I enjoy cooking, or is it just a necessary part of entertaining?
- Do I entertain often at home?
- Do I cook for family often?
- Am I an extrovert?
- Do I feel confident in front of an audience?
- Am I interested in learning more about barbequing?
- How many people do I want to cater for?
- Do I want to grill all year round?
- Where will I put a barbeque, how much room is there, and where will I store it when it is not in use?
- What kind of location will the barbeque be in: garden, patio, balcony?
- Will I put a lot of effort into maintenance, or do I want easy clean?
- What kind of fuel do I prefer: gas or wood or charcoal?
- How much do I want to spend?

You need to give yourself honest answers ... if you are shy and feel nervous about cooking, that doesn't mean you shouldn't buy a barbeque, but perhaps you should give yourself a year to get used to it before asking everyone you know around for a meal.

If you love to cook, and you feel you will use the barbeque every day in summer, and any fine day at any other time of the year, then plan to shop for a high quality sturdy outdoor kitchen. If it's just the odd 'do' then functional and easy might be the way to go.

The structure

- The grilling unit should be held by a sturdy, safe construction.
- Ensure that the hood is well attached and not wobbly and wheels are large and strong, with brakes, and the barbeque is easy to move.
- The total unit should not be top heavy and the assembly should be straightforward.
- Check what the warranty covers, and whether the brand offers after sales service and spare parts.
- Look out for sharp edges and awkward handling.

The price is right

Don't buy on price. When my wife buys clothes she 'prices' them herself by dividing the price by the number of times she thinks she will wear an outfit. Thus a £20 'bargain' that would be worn once is much more expensive than the £100 item she will wear every week. I have to admit, it's a good system. So 'price' your barbeque. Use it every day for three months? That seemingly expensive outdoor kitchen is suddenly much better value for money. Once a year? The 'end of season special' you like the price of turns out to be more expensive than you think.

I'm a man. Men cook outside. Women make the three-bean salad. That's the way it is and always has been. That outdoor grilling is a manly pursuit has long been beyond question. If this wasn't firmly understood, you'd never get grown men to put on those aprons with pictures of dancing wienies and things on the front ...

William Geist, The New York Times

Fuel & starters

chapter 3
Fuel and starters

Wood

This is how barbequing started. Men and women have gathered around burning wood for warmth, food and safety for thousands of years. And while we've learned better ways to stay safe and warm, that wood-smoke cooked meat flavour still attracts us, and is hard to beat, even with all our modern indoor appliances. Hardwood does have its drawbacks. It burns faster than charcoal or briquettes, so isn't completely suited to cooking projects that need a lot of time. It is an extra hassle to be restocking the barbeque during cooking, and you lose heat and add more to cooking time. Also the fire has to be started quite a long time before you intend to cook, as flames have to die down. Hardwood is suited to open barbeques and horizontal barrel-style smokers. However, the flavour may well be worth the effort.

Like it and lump it

Lumpwood charcoal is wood that has been fired in a kiln. It is very black, very light and ignites very easily. It is basically wood that has already been burnt to the charcoal stage, so you don't have the waiting around that you do with hardwood. When you buy lumpwood charcoal, look for large pieces, small bits are of little use, and it should be large enough to burn for a prolonged period.

Lumpwood benefits

An advantage of lumpwood charcoal is that it can be easily impregnated with a lighting agent to speed up the lighting process. No other firelighters are needed. Needless to say, add your lighting agent before igniting, and DO NOT try adding it later, when flames are present, if the fire seems a 'bit slow'. It isn't the fire that's a bit slow.

Super griller and the briquettes

Sounds like a great show, and it will be. Briquettes are an excellent heat source and are easy to use. Good quality briquettes are crushed charcoal with added starch. The best for heat are made from crushed coconut shells. Not only do these produce more kilowatts but they also hold their heat for longer. The cheaper and sometimes heavier briquettes on the market can contain useless fillers, such as sand, sawdust, or anthracite. They smell bad when lit, and don't give you anything for their extra weight.

Gas: excellent before the meal, not so good after!

Got gas? Might as well, it's easy, safe and clean. Seriously attractive reasons to use gas for barbequing. There are two types of bottled gas: propane and butane. A mixture of the two is used in Australia and New Zealand, but in colder conditions, such as often occurs in summer in the Northern Hemisphere, propane will be better than butane. Natural gas can be used, but requires special fittings.

For ease of use, speed and quick shut down, gas is the best fuel. What you lose is flavour, but wood chips can bring back the woody open-flame, man-cooked food flavour.

COME ON BABY, LIGHT MY FIRE
For safety and everyone's comfort, buy a purpose made firelighter. Put the kerosene and petrol away! Leave the cheapo fire cube things in the bargain store where they belong. BBQ firelighters do not contain paraffin, they are solid and safe. They do not sting your eyes with fumes, nor taint your food; they do not singe your eyebrows or flambé your face. Set the firelighters under your fuel, with gaps to allow air to circulate. Light. The characteristic smell will be gone long before you cook.

Fire lighter fluid

Use BEFORE you light the fire. I didn't really need to say it, did I? Impregnate lumpwood charcoal, or pour a little over your fuel. Close the lid on the container, put well away from the barbeque, and out of the reach of children. Then, and only then, ignite fuel with a long stemmed match or gas match. NEVER add more once the fire is started. Do I need to mention that again?

Fire lighter gel

Cold gels that can really hot things up! These lighting aids are thick, flammable gels that are squeezed onto dry fuel and then ignited. They are quick to start a fire, but can be tricky to use. Safe responsible use is the order of the day. Do not smear it on your hands and perform the dance of the flaming idiot. Put it on your fuel before igniting; NEVER add more once the fire has started. Keep it away from heat, children and any idiot friends you might have invited round for a fun evening.

At the flick of a switch

Electric fire starters might lack the glamour of other fire starters, but they are certainly the most easy to use, safe and reliable. Many gas BBQs have automatic starters, but for briquette or charcoal barbeques an electric fire starter is an optional extra. They look just like a portable element on an electric cord with a plug. And that is exactly what they are. Place the element in among the charcoal or briquettes, plug in, switch on and it will do the rest. Do not leave unattended, and remember to put out of harm's way after you remove it from your barbeque. It will remain hot for some time afterwards, so don't leave it lying on your French-polished rosewood dining table, or near little fingers.

Safety, cleaning & hygiene

chapter 4
Safety, cleaning & hygiene

Bugs-r-off!

Beautiful hot summer afternoons and long summer evenings: perfect for cooking outdoors. Perfect for unwelcome winged guests: flies, sand flies, midges and mozzies ... Keep all your food covered. And remember to cover it after it's cooked, while it rests. (This also keeps spills, ash and the odd splash of beer from 'marinating' your ingredients!). Food covers, clean dry tea towels, gauze, plastic wrap, and foil are all good covers. Foil is good for hot foods that are resting, as it serves the dual purpose of retaining heat and keeping the bugs off.

Keep 'em handy

How long are your arms? That's as far as you want to go from your BBQ once you get cooking. Think about what utensils you will need before you start, and arrange them all within reach. Keep all bottles and jars on a flat surface, have knives in a safe spot within reach, do not hang anything over the grill or hot area above your BBQ, or anywhere that would have you reaching across heat to retrieve it. And be sure all safety requirements (extinguisher, salt, water) are also nearby. Don't delegate preparation of the utensils and equipment you will need, get it all ready yourself, that way when you want it—and you probably will, quite suddenly—you will know it is there, exactly where you put it.

KEEPING TOES INTACT

Charcoal is hot. Knives are sharp. Cooks can be clumsy. The last thing your guests want is to spend the evening carrying the chef off to the emergency room to have a six-inch carving knife extracted from his foot. So as warm as the weather is, leave the sandals for later, and while you cook, wear covered shoes. Obvious, isn't it?

Keep close and watch

Never, ever leave the barbeque unattended. Have everything you need handy before you begin. Ask a friend to get you anything you've forgotten, and don't leave until the charcoal is out, the briquettes quelled or gas turned off. I'll say it again: never ever leave the barbeque unattended.

Sharpen up

Here's some advice that sticks out like a sore thumb: any knife is dangerous, but none so risky as a blunt knife. Blunt knives slide off rather than cut through, and your finger might be the closest thing to that blunt blade. Keep your knives sharp. Invest in a high quality steel or have them professionally sharpened. And remember to take care with a brand new knife – it is the sharpest it will ever be.

Keep the home fire not burning

You could rely on the fire brigade to douse any disasters, but prevention is better than any cure, and keeping your BBQ well maintained will go a long way to preventing flare-ups and potential house fires. But add armour to your arsenal by keeping a fire extinguisher, a bucket of water and a container of salt on standby. These are tools to tackle any fires before they get out of hand. A fat flare up under the grill can be dealt with by tossing a handful of salt onto the burning fluid. More serious threatening flames should be tackled by turning off the gas, a good amount of water or, as a last resort, your fire extinguisher. Forget your dinner, and your ego, if it looks dangerous and you can't get close enough to close the hood, don't hesitate: put it out.

Lock up the livestock

You don't have to be Michael Douglas to know that the family bunny is not recommended as the main course. Avoid distressing incidents by keeping pets, and children of course, well clear of the barbeque area.

Cool it before bed!

Letting the party hot up after the meal is one thing, but setting the patio alight is quite another. The best way to leave a lasting impression is with the quality of your food, not a close call escape from an inferno. Once the party is over, or at least your role as chef is complete, ensure all charcoal and briquettes are dead. Don't leave the barbeque area until the heat is off, and let your friends enjoy the warm glow of your hospitality.

Tuck in

Loose lips might lose wars, but at the barbeque loose clothing turns you into a flaming martyr to basic barbeque safety hazards. And no doubt your friend with the video camera will be selling footage to TV, or posting it on the internet, within a week. Keep clothing tucked in, no flapping aprons, long hair or loose shirt-tails dangling over the flames.

Putting out a fire with gasoline

A bad idea? Spraying oil onto directly grilling food is another bad idea, producing similar results, but people still seem hell bent on doing it! We all want the food smoky, but let's not turn it into charcoal. And let's not have a few layers of skin singed off into the bargain.

Quick tip

BRUSH-UP ON SAFETY

No one likes cleaning, and nine out of ten guys will boast that they never clean the barbeque. Nine out of ten guys will also have experienced a close call fire hazard type of disaster! Dirty barbeques are like dry forests, just waiting for lightning to strike. Keeping the barbeque clean is an essential part of your safety procedure, and it only takes a few minutes. So, just allow a few minutes at either end of the barbeque time to give the grill a quick brushing with a good wire brush, and clean out the drip tray. That's all. Done. Easy isn't it?

Top 10

safety tips

- **Apron** – This will keep any bits of dangling clothing from coming in contact with the cooking area and provide a first line of defence against hot splashes or ash.

- **A clean barbeque** – Both from a food safety angle and also no nasty surprises from old fat flaming up.

- **Even surface** – Make sure any barbeque is on a flat, level surface to prevent hot things sliding off.

- **Good lighting** – You have to see what you are cooking and make sure it isn't you!

- **Mitten or oven gloves** – It's easy to forget how hot things are when they come off the grill, especially tools.

- **No children or pets** – Unless you want to invent a new recipe, keep all kids well out of the way and all pets indoors.

- **No overhanging plants & trees** – Some plants have volatile sap and can easily catch fire. Even green stems can soon dry out and ignite over a barbeque.

- **Shoes** – Slip-ons are best as there are no laces to come undone and trip over. Avoid open sandals and slippers.

- **Use lighting fluid carefully** – Only use on cold charcoal, NEVER on hot coals.

- **Water and/or fire extinguisher at hand** – Just in case! Make sure the extinguisher is topped up and is within easy reach.

Raincoats

Sure, it's designed for outdoor use, but leaving your barbeque outdoors in all weather all year round is as sensible as leaving your car exposed to wind, rain and snow 365 days a year. A simple canvas cover, plastic sheeting tied over it, or, ideally, storing it in a shed through the winter months will give you many more years of use, and less maintenance. Just a note, don't put the cover on until the barbeque is cold.

Foiled

Do you know anyone who lines the grill bed with foil? It isn't a short cut to a cleaner barbeque; it's a potential danger. So don't waste money, time or the risk of singed eyebrows, face and dignity. The barbeque is designed to work without additions, and cleaning is easy enough. Leave loose bits of metal that will disintegrate in your barbie's heat out of the way. Save it to wrap a fish in.

Cleaning the gas barbeque

Five main areas to clean:

- Grill surfaces (either grill or plate).
- Flame tamers.
- Elements.
- Drip trays.
- Structure.

GRILL SURFACE

Use a scraper and wire brush straight after the barbeque while the grill or plate is still hot.

For enamel grills use only a copper brush.

Use a scraper mainly to clean the plate.

Prevent rusting by oiling the cast iron grill after cleaning.

Clean thoroughly in soapy water every two or three months depending on usage.

FLAME TAMERS

In most good quality barbeques you can find a layer of flame tamers between the elements and the grill. These flame tamers could be made from steel, cast iron or could exist out of a layer of lava rocks or ceramic rocks. Weber gas barbeques have steel flavour bars.

It is very important to keep this section of the barbeque clean to avoid flare-ups.

Clean cast iron and steel flame tamers with a wire brush and occasionally wash in soapy water. Lava rocks and ceramic rocks should be self-cleaning. Leave barbeque on hot after you've grilled and the fats should burn off. Occasionally pour water over these rocks while hot and wash with detergent in hot water every few months depending on usage. These rocks will eventually build up with so much grease and fat that they have to be replaced. Weber flavour bars are easy to clean.

ELEMENTS

Elements are made from cast iron or stainless steel. Depending on the construction the holes in the elements could gradually fill up with fat and grease and the uneven gas flow will cause hot and cold spots on the grilling surface. Take elements off and clean the holes with a brush. If really blocked, soak in very hot water with detergent and dry in the oven. Cast iron elements can be covered with a film of oil after cleaning to slow down rust.

THE DRIP TRAY

This part can cause the most serious flare up if not cleaned properly. A thick layer of fat can cause some spectacular fires and ruin food. Clean this part and use a barbeque fat-absorbing product to reduce the chance of flare-ups.

STRUCTURE

Try to keep the barbeque clean not only for looks but especially to keep the flies and other little pests away. Don't feed them by leaving food stuck to the barbeque.

Don't forget to keep the inside of the hood clean.

Orange appeal

Here's a great tip for helping to clean a barbecue grill. Wait until grill gets fairly hot. Slice an orange in half. Take the sliced orange and rub on grill racks. Make sure to wear gloves. Works like a charm.

Boys' toys!

chapter 5
Boys' toys!

Hey, we call them tools, not toys.

After the Big One, the barbeque, a bloke's got to have a few extras, and no, they are not 'toys' they are tools!

Knives

A good quality knife does much of the work.

A speciality cooking equipment shop will offer an enormous variety of knives, and advice. A good knife kit should include the basic Gang of Four: chef's knife, boning knife, paring knife and serrated knife.

- Chef's knife – multi purpose for cutting meat, dicing, chopping, julienne, carving.
- Boning knife – stripping sinew off meat, de-boning.
- Paring knife – preparing vegetables, peeling.
- Serrated knife – cutting bread, vegetables.

Sharpening systems

When you have knives, you need to maintain them. A good quality knife is a significant investment, and an item you should be using daily. So keep it in good nick by sharpening regularly. You can use a stone, a commercial sharpener and a steel to keep the edge. Or have it professionally sharpened regularly.

Chimney starters

These are a great way to get a charcoal grill going, as they considerably speed up the process. A chimney is a metal cylinder with a heat-proof handle and a grate to hold the charcoal. Put one or two fire starters on the centre of your barbeque, place the chimney over the top and fill with charcoal. Light the starters, and in less than 20 minutes the coals will be red, protected from wind, but well ventilated in the chimney. Grasp the handle and carefully tip the coals into the barbeque. Arrange them for heat distribution, direct or indirect grilling.

Internal meat thermometer

Definitely a must when grilling large items of meat or poultry and extremely important when spit roasting whole animals and large cuts. This item consists of a long probe approximately 150mm (6") long and a thermometer at the end. Some thermometers have indications of required internal temperatures for the different types of meat and poultry. Before the grilling process begins insert the probe in the thickest part of the meat without touching the bone. Then just check the reading when the cooking time is nearly up.

The required internal temperatures:

- Beef 60°C/140°F rare, 71°C/160°F medium, 77°C/170°F well done.
- Veal 77°C/170°F.
- Lamb 80°C/175°F well done.
- Pork 85°C/185°F.
- Poultry 88°C/190°F.

BRUSH UP

Keep the barbeque clean with a good steel wire brush.
As menacing as this thing looks, it makes easy work of
the grime, grease and charred-on food of the barbeque.

Scrapers

A good strong firm handled scraper will keep the grill plates
clean. As with wire brushes, use it before everything congeals.

BBQ brushes

These look like paintbrushes, and do something similar. They
carry the marinade, or moisture to the food. But remember,
whatever you are brushing, be it hot food or hot grills, do so
quickly! Being slow will result in a dramatically shortened
bristle. I don't need to tell you that these are rendered useless,
and trying to extinguish your marinating brush basically makes
you look like a fool. So, quick brushstrokes – be Picasso, not
Rembrandt!

Roasting baskets

Fish, vegetables, duck, sausages ... all can be easily cooked
in specially designed hinged baskets that enclose the food,
and can be flipped, a bit like an old fashioned toast rack.
Most are stainless steel and easy to clean.

Longer is better

Barbeque shops sell special barbeque utensils with extra long handles. There is a reason: you want to cook the eye fillet, not yourself. Long handled utensils are to be recommended, not only to save the cook from a scorching, but also to make the food easily accessible and enable quick removal from the grill when it's done. Many a good steak has become charred as a BBQ chef hunts down a utensil to get the meat off the grill. Don't improvise, have the right utensil, have it handy, and use it.

The art of timing

Just like comedy, the art of barbequing hinges on timing. Keep a clock with a minute hand near the barbeque. And don't ever rely on your friends as timekeepers ... that beer in the fridge or attractive girl by the pool can send the thought of a medium rare roast eye fillet right out of the best-intentioned timekeeper's head.

Tongs tongs tongs!

Tongs. Not meat forks. Is this clear enough? Every time a cut of meat, and likely an expensive one, is stabbed with a curious fork, it loses juice. The idea of barbequing is to keep the most moisture IN. Stop the stabbing now!

Get your mitts on

A good thick oven mitt or glove is invaluable ... blistered fingers make it hard to eat. Grabbing the grill, or even the meat off the grill in an emergency, requires adequate protection for tender fingertips. Mitts are not womanly or old-fashioned, they are less undignified than learning to juggle with something really hot.

Quick tip

GETTING BOARD?

Barbeque, knife, ingredients, you in a fancy-looking apron. What else could you need? A chopping board. A good quality heavy-duty board is worth its weight in BBQ food. A good chopping board is the team mate to the knife. You won't ruin an outdoor table, or damage an expensive knife, and it looks professional too! Keep it clean by washing or salting, and remember to prevent cross-contamination of food by using one side for meats and the other for fruits and vegetables. Better yet, have several boards, each designated for either raw meats or fruits and vegetables.

The thermometer at the end of your arm

Most commercial gas barbeques have built in thermometers on the hood, but charcoal or briquette burning barbeques usually don't. Gauging temperatures on these is easy just by using your hand. No, don't TOUCH the grill ... charred fingertips might indicate high temperature, but are hardly conducive to the end result of a good meal, or impressed guests. But a hand hovering at the right distance from the grill can be an accurate indicator of heat. Hold your hand, palm open, just above the grill and count the seconds before you pull your hand away. (NB there are no prizes for record breakers – remember, you want an accurate idea of the heat).

Very Hot	2–3 seconds
Hot	3–4 seconds
Medium	4–6 seconds
Cool	6 seconds or more

Cook it through

The one golden rule of safe barbecuing is to cook your food right the way through. Exposed to a very high heat, food will brown—even blacken—very quickly, but that doesn't necessarily mean the centre is cooked.

One way to find out is to simply cut to the centre and check it's colour – if your chicken, pork, sausages, burgers or kebabs are at all pink in the middle, leave them grilling. If you don't want to spoil the presentation of your food by making a large incision, there are meat thermometers available that help you determine when your food is fully cooked.

Introducing
flavour

chapter 6
Introducing flavour

For more than massage ...

Oil: the perfect medium for flavour. Infused oils are easily spread onto food and do double work, lubricating the food so it won't stick to the grill and delivering the essence you've added. Especially good for infusing flavour into oil are garlic cloves (squashed, not crushed), fresh rosemary, whole chillies (slice in half for stronger flavour), citrus peel, or essential oils (take care to avoid using essential oils that are too fragrant – you don't want the food to taste like perfume!). Add a spoonful of high quality sesame oil to a cheaper, lighter peanut or canola oil to impart flavour and spare cost. Apply with a BBQ brush.

Quick tip

TO EVERY MEAL THERE IS A SEASONING
Be a man for all seasonings. Don't just stick to good old salt and pepper, as useful as they are. Branch out with coarse sea salt, smoked salts, freshly ground black pepper, pink peppercorns, lemon pepper, Szechwan pepper, green peppercorns. Try something new or different combinations of old favourites.

When to use dried herbs

Use dried herbs for rubs used during direct grilling. Fresh herbs burn readily and become bitter, giving off a garden-fire aroma that is, well, not exactly appetising. Dried herbs have a stronger taste, too, so you don't need to use as much for an equal burst of taste.

Marinate

Marinades tenderise, moisten and flavour meat. To tenderise meat use acids found in fruit juices (lemon, lime, pineapple, pomegranate) in vinegar (wine, rice wine, sherry, cider, balsamic vinegar) or in cultured milk products such as yogurt. To moisturise use oils or alcohol (rice wines, sake, wine, sherry, beer), to flavour use anything from herbs, spices, honey, soy sauce, chilli sauce, Tabasco, wasabi. Try to balance sweet, sour and salt and sometimes bitter. Be aware of the time food is marinated – over-marinating can ruin many ingredients, so consult the recipe for guidelines.

Quick tip

PLASTIC FANTASTIC

It's in the bag. A couple of tablespoons of your favourite marinade, throw in the ingredients, tie the top and shake it all around. Return to fridge, and turn the bag occasionally, until marinating time is up. Remove the food, and throw away the bag. Quick, easy, clean ... the three magic words.

Don't come on too strong

The rule for marinades is the same as the rule for aftershave.
You aren't disguising something, you're enhancing it.
Too long in the marinade and that's all you will taste, with
a loss of texture to boot. Light delicate flavours need little
enhancement; older tougher cuts need a bit more help. Just
like us, when you think about it. So, easy on the Old Spice
and the meat spice.

DRIP DRY
Before adding marinated meats to the barbeque allow
excess oil to drip off, otherwise the danger of an oil flare
up is likely. The oil should have done its job of moisturising
a drier cut of meat, and allowing the excess to run off will
not reduce the effect it's already had.

Rub a dub

A rub is one of the easiest ways to add to the taste of your
main ingredient. Meats are easily spiced up or given a delicate
aromatic zing with a good rub. No, I don't mean massaging the
fillet or doing physiotherapy on your chicken thigh. A rub is
a balanced combination of herbs, spices and seasonings that
enhance the flavour of the food or create the taste of a regional
cuisine. Applied as a mixture of dry ingredients this is called
a dry rub. These are easy to make, easy to store, easy to use
and impart a big increase in flavour.

Top 10

spices

- **Aniseed** – Sweet and very aromatic with liquorice taste.
- **Cardamon** – eucalyptus, camphor with lemony undertone.
- **Chilli** – refers to the small, hot types of capsicum.
- **Chinese five spice** – sweet, sour, bitter, savory, and salty!
- **Cinnamon** – available ground or in sticks (quills).
- **Cloves** – aromatic dried flower buds of a tree.
- **Coriander (ground)** – dried seeds of the coriander herb.
- **Cumin** – draws out the natural sweetness of dishes.
- **Nutmeg** – seed of the evergreen nutmeg tree.
- **Paprika** – ground, dried sweet red bell peppers.

herbs

- **Basil** – use fresh and add at last moment.
- **Garlic** – pungent but mellows and sweetens with cooking.
- **Lemongrass** – finely slice or bruise the stems and add whole.
- **Mint** – try different flavours like apple, ginger or pineapple.
- **Oregano** – an aromatic, warm and slightly bitter taste.
- **Parsley** – flat leaved varieties have a stronger flavour.
- **Rosemary** – complements oily foods, such as lamb and fish.
- **Sage** – slight peppery and used for flavouring fatty meats.
- **Tarragon** – aromatic property reminiscent of anise.
- **Thyme** – best herb for retaining its flavour when dried.

Wet and wildly tasty

Wet rub: sounds good, doesn't it? Okay, out of the spa and back to the kitchen. A wet rub is a combination of fresh herbs, spices, and seasonings with a liquid base. Garlic, onion, fresh herbs, citrus juice, oils can all be ingredients of a wet rub. A wet rub gives you good control of the resulting flavours.

A little bit of chutney, a little bit of salsa

Chutneys and salsas: make your own. This is easy cooking, and can be prepared in advance. Chutney recipes abound and can be made in winter in preparation for the summer barbeque season. Salsas can be whipped up a few hours before use. Interesting combinations like pineapple, coriander and chilli or mango chunks with fresh ginger and lime zest can really give a zing to your food and require no cooking at all. And they look colourful and fresh.

A chip off the old block

Wood chips are a simple way to add a lot of flavour to your cooking. A variety are available from your local barbeque supplier, or some hardware stores. To get the most flavour from wood chips always soak the quantity you need for 50 minutes beforehand in water. Drain well. Then add to white-hot coals or in the smoking box of your outdoor kitchen.

Aye, there's the rub

Dry rub: a good dry rub is made up of, wait for it, all dry ingredients! Its not rocket science, but it can be an explosion of interesting flavours in the mouth. Tantalise taste buds with warm, hot, spicy, salty dry rubs. A word of warning: find a few good recipes and work with them before you branch out and experiment with your own.

Spice of life

Aromatic smoking ingredients are simple to obtain, and are likely to be already growing in your garden or lolling about in your fruit bowl. Citrus peel, kaffir lime leaves and even pineapple skins (use the flesh for dessert) give excellent flavour-enhancing smoke. Spices like cloves, star anise, and cinnamon sticks placed on the coals create deep fragrant smoky flavoured smoke. Add a handful of tea leaves, fruit or herb tea.

Spice up the taste of that pork loin or lamb rack with a handful of spice ... no, not on the meat, on the flames. Star anise, cloves, cinnamon quills, or whole nutmegs on hot coals will infuse your meats with an exotic warm smoky flavour. Combine your spicy smoke with an Eastern style marinade and the results will be exotically delicious.

Planning &
attitude

chapter 7
Planning & attitude

Plan ahead

It's great to have a spontaneous dinner, but as casual as barbequing is, don't make the mistake of going at it without pre-planning. Make a timeline that includes shopping, cleaning your equipment, getting your gas bottle filled (or charcoal burning), guests' arrival time, cooking, and menu timing.
The ten minutes you spend on this will pay off when your food arrives at the table perfectly cooked, and before your friends have sent out for pizza!

Quick tip

GET IN LINE!
Writing out a quick timeline for your barbeque is an easy way to keep things on schedule and running smoothly.
It's the old story of a little planning going a long way.
You don't need to be pedantic about it, just a few words to remind you what you need to do, a bit like a shopping list, will suffice.

Sample timeline

Imagine a barbeque for ten guests on Saturday evening:

Menu – grilled salmon with horseradish, mustard and rum as entrée (see recipe), roasted stuffed rib eye steak, and grilled pineapple with fresh ginger and rum (see recipe).

Entrée served on baguette, main course accompanied by tossed salad and small gourmet potatoes in herb butter, and pineapple served with ice cream.

Times: 6.00pm guests arrive, drinks, entrée at 7.00pm, main course 7.45pm and dessert at 8.45pm.

Equipment – a four-burner gas barbeque with hood.

Thursday/Friday

- Shopping – buy meats, fruits, salads, etc., check the pantry for everything else you will need, i.e. oil, seasonings, sugar, and add anything missing to your list. Double check!
- Fuel – fill gas bottle.
- Clean BBQ.

Saturday a.m.

- Prepare dressing for salmon (2 minutes) see recipe.
- Open 2.4–2.8 kg (5–6lbs) rib eye fillet and take out all sinew and fat with a sharp boning knife (or have your butcher do this), stuff cavity with sautéed mushrooms, garlic and seasoning. Tie meat with butcher's twine (15 minutes).
- Make the sauce for the pineapple (10 minutes) see recipe.
- Prepare 2 pineapples and coat the wedges with the sauce (15 minutes) see recipe.

Saturday p.m.

- 5.00 pm prepare potatoes, herb butter and tossed salad.
- 5.30 pm prepare bar for drinks.
- 6.00 pm welcome guests and serve drinks.
- 6.15 pm preheat gas barbeque.
- 6.20 pm place rib eye in barbeque and indirect grill at 180–220°C (350–420°F).
- 6.35 pm coat salmon side with dressing and slice baguettes at an angle, 13mm (½") thickness.
- 6.45 pm place salmon side next to rib eye and indirect grill for 15 minutes and boil potatoes on side burner or stove.
- 7.00 pm remove salmon from barbeque and serve on sliced baguettes.
- 7.20 pm check on potatoes and prepare the tossed salad, mustard and other condiments.
- 7.35 pm turn gas off, cut string off rib eye, cover with foil and allow meat to rest for 10 minutes.
- 7.45 pm serve main course.
- 8.20pm restart the barbeque.
- 8.25 pm place pineapple on barbeque and indirect grill for 15 minutes.
- 8.40 pm reheat caramel sauce on side burner or stove.
- 8.45 pm serve a quarter pineapple per person with sauce and ice cream.
- Turn off the barbeque!

Trial runs are worth the effort

Don't test out the new recipe, or barbeque, on sixty guests. Trial run recipes and equipment for everyone's sake! Having a 'honeymoon' period to get to know your barbeque may sound corny, but every instrument has its idiosyncrasies, and the barbeque is no exception. Variations from model to model will make a difference to your cooking: faster, slower, higher heat, even the ease of opening and closing the hood should all be tested out on trial runs with the family or a few patient friends.

Trying out recipes a few times also helps a great deal. Some cookbooks prove to have vital pieces of info missing when it comes to putting it all together, and the confidence you will exude when you are sure of the recipe will help your guests and you have a more enjoyable and relaxed BBQ experience. Remember, opening night is always the culmination of many rehearsals.

Take note of the weather

You need to have weather information, not just to protect your guests from a downpour, but to help you in cooking their meal. The recipe says indirect grill for one hour. But there's a strong breeze nipping round the back of the barbeque … and three hours later someone has driven off to get a curry. Always allow for weather conditions to alter cooking times. A strong wind will slow down your barbeque, be it gas or charcoal. Plan for the conditions, and get things cooking ahead of time if it gets gusty.

Develop an attitude!

Why limit yourself to boring old barbeque menus and traditional dishes? Use your imagination. BBQ bread – why not? A hooded charcoal barbeque is basically a wood fired oven, perfect for Italian style breads and pizza. On our camping holidays my wife bakes bread after dinner, when there is still heat left in the charcoal, and we treat ourselves to fresh hot bread for supper. Gas barbeques are excellent for baking bread. With either charcoal or gas, the bread must be grilled indirect. Dough can be mixed in a bread baker, or mixer with a dough hook attachment, but really it is so quick and easy to make dough by hand you don't need fancy equipment. Once the dough has proved, put it either in a pan or directly onto the oiled grill. Cover and cook. Pizzas are popular with everyone, and suit the casual barbeque meal atmosphere. Have all the toppings ready on hand, and just make up the pizza as you go. As a starter a pizza or fresh focaccia bread take the edge off hunger, and then the main meal can roast away quietly as you enjoy dips, spreads or flavoured butters on crusty fresh home baked bread.

Dear diary …

Do you remember your first (and hopefully last) barbeque disaster? No? Well, you should do. Make notes about all your experiences. A short diary entry can save you from harm and embarrassment and add to your expertise and knowledge. Watch what other cooks do, note what works, and what doesn't. Jot down a few recipes, innovations and barbeque tips gleaned from your own and others' experiences to aid your memory and expertise.

Top 10

basic food safety tips

- Always check food on freshness (looks and smell).
- Clean grill surface straight after grilling.
- Continuously wipe and wash boards and barbeque utensils.
- Cover food while bringing to room temperature or while resting meats after grilling.
- Don't reuse marinades.
- Ensure the grill surface is clean.
- Grill poultry, pork & lamb till thoroughly cooked (don't half cook).
- Separate raw foods from cooked.
- Use different carving boards for cooked and raw food and poultry.
- Use different knives for preparing cooked and raw food and poultry or wash the knives well before moving to another type of food.
- Wash hands regularly.

Light your fire!

So you know how long to cook your steak, you have top quality meat, and you are looking at a slavering crowd of hungry mates. Save yourself time, and embarrassment, and remember to PREHEAT the grill. Nearly all instructions and cooking times indicate the cooking time from adding food to the grill when the grill has reached the designated maximum temperature. If your recipe instructs you to "Cook on high heat for 20 minutes" then the grill needs to be at high before adding the food, then cook for the required twenty minutes.

An ounce of preparation …

The drinks are flowing, the party is warming up, but the barbeque isn't. Don't forget to have enough fuel for your cooking needs. Fill gas bottles or stock up on charcoal the day before. It can be a long and boring evening if you spend it at a gas station instead of at the party. And as is the usual case, the fuel runs out just before the meal, on a Bank Holiday, and none can be bought for love or money. The most embarrassed barbequer is the one queuing at the chippie for dinner at 9pm.

Leave it alone!

Curiosity killed the cat, and it undercooked the barbeque food too. Don't lift the hood 'just to check'. Trust your cooking times, and leave the food alone. Every lifted lid is volumes of heat released, and many minutes added to the cooking time.

Stand your ground

Keeping near the barbeque is an essential safety requirement, but it also puts you in the ideal situation to protect your food from friends who want to grandstand their own cooking skills. Nearly every bloke wants to lift the lid to take a peek or flip a steak to show he's got what it takes. Grip your tongs firmly, frown and defend your food. No one, but no one, touches your barbeque but you!

Quick tip

KEEP COOL, CALM, COLLECTED
Plan your menu to suit yourself. Don't focus on impressing your guests with fancy flambé and elaborate last minute concoctions. Plan carefully so that most of your preparation can be done well before guests arrive, with only the grilling to be completed in front of your visitors. Then you can enjoy socialising, and impress them with the calm and ease with which you produce a full meal from your barbeque.

Familiarity breeds ... expertise

Planning to cook for a crowd? Make sure you 'know' the barbeque you use. Every barbeque, even those of the same make, has its own little peculiarities and quirks. If you can, use your own, if not, trial run the equipment first. Get to know it, and when you've warmed up to each other, then, and only then, you can go on and have a big night together.

Feel confident, but don't fake it

Learn what you need to know about BBQ safety and cooking. Test your menu beforehand, get good quality ingredients, and fuel up before guests arrive. Then the air of confidence you exude will be genuine, not faked. All that earlier bravado is embarrassing when something goes wrong, but quiet confidence will keep your guests secure, and if there are delays or problems, they won't worry, knowing you will have it all in hand.

The BBQ brag

Everyone has one. A loud friend, the one who positions himself near the BBQ with a pint in hand, and loudly critiques your cooking. He'll weigh into you for your technique—or lack of—and recite old stories everyone has heard before about his own BBQ prowess. The first piece of advice when dealing with this type is, don't invite him. But hey, he's probably your brother-in-law and you have to ask him, so here's what to do. Tell everyone you're going to provide the perfect steak. Then turn to your big-mouthed friend, hand him the tongs and a large steak and tell him he can be the first. (This works best if you know how to cook the perfect steak!). When he declines, or proceeds and it goes wrong, step in and quietly, confidently take over. If, as might happen (but it is unlikely), he turns out to be a fine barbequer, relax, sit back and enjoy the company while someone else cooks you the perfect steak.

Hot plate

Think about it, how would it affect you, just when you are getting, well, nice and hot, to jump into a really cold shower? Yeah, you've got the picture; so don't throw your perfectly cooked, perfectly hot steak onto a cold slab of crockery. Preheat your plate, so the steak coming off the barbeque stays at optimum heat for the diner.

Any place, any weather

Barbeques come in all shapes and sizes and, contrary to common belief, they are suitable for year round use in a variety of locations. As a student in the South of Holland I had a small attic apartment. The tiny window overlooking the street provided a ledge wide enough to accommodate my little Hibachi grill. I would place this out of the window in all weather and grill chicken for dinner. My mother often did the same on her small balcony. Rain or shine, the aroma of Indonesian roast chicken – ayam pangang – would waft across the neighbourhood. My eldest son has been seen perched on rooftops in Europe grilling all manner of foods in all kinds of weather, so the grill gene is clearly strong in my family!

> **DID YOU KNOW?**
> Kansas City, USA hosted the world's largest barbecue in 1975. An enormous pit was dug just for the event and they roasted five bulls. It took three days and took three teams of BBQ masters.

Smoking, steak & fish

chapter 8
Smoking, steak & fish

Wood chips on gas BBQs

Gas BBQs are convenient in so many ways, but the main criticism of them is the lack of traditional smoky BBQ flavour that we associate with barbeque cooking. Adding wood chips will impart that delicious smoke, and in a relatively quick and easy way. Commercial wood smoke boxes are available at BBQ specialist shops, but an easy home made version will do the job just as well. Make some aluminium foil parcels by using a double layer of foil, filled with wet wood chips. Make a few holes in the top to allow the smoke to escape and place the parcel on the element of your gas barbeque under the grill. This should be done at the early stage of cooking, when the meat is still raw, allowing the flavour enhancing smoke to really permeate the meat.

Where there is smoke, there is flavour

There isn't much point in barbequing if it isn't adding something to your food's flavour. Adding wood chips to your barbeque is an easy way to introduce a smoky flavour to meats and vegetables. Specialist barbeque shops stock a variety of different pre-packaged wood chips. Recommended varieties include hickory, maple, mesquite, alder and oak barrel chips. An American favourite is Jack Daniels wood chips. But whatever your choice of wood chip, the addition of some 'real' barbeque flavour will make the world of difference to the end result.

The gardener's BBQ tip

Homemade wood chips are as inexpensive and as easy to acquire as the old fruit tree branches you pruned off the tree in your garden. Apple, peach, cherry are all excellent varieties for smoking. Cut the wood into chips and chunks and store in a dry place until they are thoroughly dried.

As crazy as it sounds, you will need to wet it before you use it. The dry wood should be soaked in water for 20–50 minutes before you add it to white-hot charcoal (or place in a smoking pan on a gas BBQ). This means it doesn't burn up too quickly, and your food gets more smoke. Use the smoke at the start of the grilling process to get maximum flavour. Don't be tempted to use the off cuts from your last DIY project. The gas given off may well be toxic and will make your food taste terrible, and your guests feel ill. And let's be eco-friendly when we grill.

Wanna smoke some herb?

Recommended smoke-producing herbs: rosemary, sage, lavender, oregano, and thyme. Note: 'wet' herbs like mint, basil, coriander and parsley are not good smoke producers. Generally herbs that prefer dry climates and have a woody stem will produce more aromatic smoke. Don't forget whole spices, either. A few cinnamon quills, or whole nutmegs will give a warm aromatic flavour. And herbs and spices on the coals giving off their sweet smoke will delight your guests and create an exotic atmosphere, and ignite anticipation of the meal to come!

Top 10

flavourings better grown than bought

- **Chives** – dies back with new leaves in spring.
- **Coriander** – does not like growing near fennel.
- **Kaffir limes** – grow in large pot on a sunny patio.
- **Lemons** – mist the leaves early morning in summer.
- **Limes** – plants will last 3 to 5 years.
- **Mint** – fast growing and does best in a clay pot.
- **Parsley** – grows in a deep pot to helps the long taproot.
- **Rosemary** – tolerates drought and cuttings root easily.
- **Sage** – grow in dry, well-drained, alkaline soil.
- **Thyme** – perennial that likes a hot, sunny, dry spot.

flavour enhancers

- **Brines** – add flavour and moisture to meat, fish & poultry.
- **Dry rubs** – a balance of herbs, spices and seasonings.
- **Flavoured butters** – good way of using up leftover fresh herbs.
- **Flavoured smoke** – try hickory, apple or mesquite.
- **Infused oil** – lubricates food and adds essence.
- **Marinates** – tenderise, moisten and flavour meat.
- **Mopping sauces** – used to baste meat whilst cooking.
- **Salt & freshly ground pepper** – try different flavours.
- **Sauces** – different ones can be made for different foods.
- **Wet rubs/pastes** – moist ingredients added to spices and herbs.

GOING AGAINST THE GRAIN

Everyone has had to chew their way through a piece of meat that seems more like the wood under the grill than the sizzling main course on it. To help keep meat tender, carve against the grain when you are preparing it and when serving it. If you are not sure, then cut a thin slice and look at the fibres of the meat. If you can see obvious strands, then that is 'with' the grain, cutting across the grain should look like meat, not strips or strings.

The perfect steak

Nothing impresses more than a perfectly cooked juicy steak; it is undoubtedly the easiest, yet most frequently ruined BBQ meal, and there are few cookery subjects that get more discussion than the 'doneness' of steak. Chefs tear their hair out as diners request 'medium/well/rare with blood but no pink, and dry on the outside, but not tough'.

Let's get this straight, the perfect steak is medium rare. That is the default setting. Learn to cook a great medium rare, and then you'll handle the well-dones, rares and blues that your guests throw at you at the last minute. So here goes ...

How to cook it

Start with a good quality rib eye, one inch thick. Have the meat at room temperature – that means don't grab it out of the fridge and slap it immediately on the grill or your timing will be all out. On the other hand don't leave the thing lying around with the flies for half an afternoon; keep to good hygiene and food safety practices. Bring your steak out of the fridge and keep covered for 20 minutes before you are ready to cook it.

Now you have your room temp. steak, brush it with oil and season with salt and pepper. Apply a dry rub if you wish.

- Set grill on HIGH. Have a clock or watch nearby to mark time.
- Direct grill steak for two minutes, then swivel it 45° to give it a nice cross-hatched grill mark. Leave for two and half minutes more.
- Do not poke, prod or stab!
- Turn over with tongs, repeat timing and swivel.
- Remove from grill and REST for two more minutes.
- Voilá, perfect steak, medium rare.

Give it a rest

After grilling, give the steak a rest for a couple of minutes to let the juices redistribute before cutting into it. A drizzle of olive oil or a pat of butter gives the steak a handsome sheen and spectacular flavour and finish.

To recap …

Now you know how to grill the perfect steak, remember these factors: weather conditions, quality of meat, thickness of cut, and required doneness. Allow for loss of heat in strong winds, so lengthen cooking times. Remember the wok rule? Thin slices of food cooked fast on high, apply the opposite for thicker meat. the thicker the cut, the longer and slower it should be cooked. If someone wants it medium well, then add to the cooking time. See the note doneness of meat tip on pages 100 & 101.

Am I blue?

Someone wants a blue steak? No problem. The most important factor here is that the meat MUST be at room temperature to begin. Blue must be cooked on a high heat, and cooked quickly. Top quality beef is essential, as with carpaccio, it must be tender and flavoursome, because cooking isn't going to add much to the taste. Grill very quickly, a minute or two maximum on each side. The centre of the steak should not be cold, but should appear raw.

Quick tip

TAKE A BREAK

Always let red meat rest. Once it is cooked, you remove it from the heat and rest to allow the juices that concentrate in the centre of the meat while cooking to redistribute through the whole steak. This also applies to large pieces of meat, for example roasts and whole fillets.

Now that's meat!

Steak, pfft! That's for beginners ... now how about a whole rib eye, or sirloin? That's an impressive item to throw nonchalantly onto your barbeque, and carve confidently for the slavering masses hovering hopefully around you. But don't make the mistake of cooking a big cut in the same way you cook a steak. Large cuts should be indirect grilled with the hood down. Prepare your meat beforehand by rubbing with spices and seasonings, or a commercial BBQ rub. Allow enough cooking time for weather conditions—wind and cold will increase cooking time—and also for peeking (every time you lift that lid, you lose heat, but you will need to look very occasionally). Grilling time should be calculated by combining weight, tenderness and thickness of meat (see grilling charts in Chapter 11). Most barbeque manuals will have a grilling schedule specific to that model. Make use of a meat thermometer to avoid failures (particularly with poultry). Once you have the cooking time calculated, fire up and go to it.

Steak a lá Jeanne d'Arc

Well-done: words that strike at the heart of the red meat loving chef or grill jockey. But as strange as it may seem to most carnivores, there are those people out there who want their meat cardboard dry and dark brown. To cook a well-done or medium/well-done steak, reduce the heat to medium high and extend cooking time. Do not turn the meat more frequently or, simply from boredom, poke at it as it cooks. Just turn once. If your guest looks alarmed when they cut into it, throw it back on the grill – underdone is better than overdone.

There's steak and there's steak

I have said it before, but I will stress this again: quality, quality, quality. You can't make a silk purse out of a sow's ear, and a bargain too young or too old sinewy cut of meat will not become a delicious meal through cooking. Save the bargains for the casserole dish.

Quick tip

DIFFERENT CUTS

Keep a record of your experiences using different cuts of meat. You know how to cook the perfect rib eye, so experiment with tenderloin, entrecote, rump steak, pork steak, lamb and venison. A rough rule is the wok rule: the thinner and more tender the meat, the less cooking required.

Preparation

If you're grilling up a steak you might want to cut off any excess fat and season with a little salt before you start. With fish filets, I like to place them in a zip lock bag with a little olive oil and herbs but you can also prepare a glaze to coat them just before grilling. Remember to bring items to room temperature before grilling.

Grilling fish

Fish can frustrate the most experienced griller or give the most satisfaction. It is horribly disappointing when the fish that the fishmonger promised on his daughter's life was fresh, sticks to your grill and refuses to release anything but a stale aroma, and your guests silently blame your cooking skills for the disaster.

Learning how to judge the freshness of fish is one of the most useful skills a barbequer—or any kind of cook—can learn.

Where possible, fish needs to be fresh, especially when grilling whole fish.

Cooking characteristics of fish

Texture:

This depends on how the fillet reacts when cooked.

Delicate fish flakes easily when cooked and should not be direct grilled unless in foil parcels.

Medium texture fish can be used for direct or indirect grilling

Firm texture fish is suitable for all grilling.

Oil Content:

Some fish have a high oil content, so if you are grilling an oily fish, i.e. salmon, reduce the amount of oil you use.

Colour:

This is important because people eat with their eyes. The colour of the fish can change after grilling.

Flavour:

Some varieties have a nice delicate flavour and not much extra flavouring is needed, while others will need marinating or flavouring.

As a general rule for barbequing, use fish with a firm texture and high oil content, especially if grilling a whole fish. Don't over-marinate the fish as the delicate nature of the texture can be easily broken, or the fish taste overpowered by marinades.

Sticky fish:

How to stop fish sticking to the grill, and avoid an undignified scraping and hacking at the food! The reason fish sticks is that the proteins oozing from the fish flesh while it is cooking stick to the grill. The answer is to make the surface slippery and cook the fish as fast as possible. Always oil the grill before placing the fish on it and use an old pot lid to cover the fish, or close the hood of your barbeque to allow the heat to circulate around the fish. It will have less chance to stick and the cooking time is greatly reduced. Another solution is to coat the fish in seasoned flour – this will reduce the sticky problem and add flavour.

Buying fish

Get your fish at the busiest fish store you can find. Chances are it will be freshest from there. Buy it as close to when you'll use it as possible and allow 200–225g (7–8oz) per person on boneless fillets and steaks. For whole fish that you will clean or cook whole, plan on 450g (1lb) per person. Frozen fish should always be thawed in your refrigerator overnight.

Freshness of fish

Fish should be stored at 0°C at all times to slow the process of deterioration.

Ask your fish retailer to put it on ice to transport it home and leave it on ice even in your refrigerator (refrigerator on 4°C). The fish will remain fresher for longer if you keep the fillets raised on a grill so that they don't sit in the juices or melted ice that run off.

Five steps to becoming the ultimate fish griller

If you are nervous about cooking fish on the barbeque, train yourself in stages. Soon you will become the gun with fish on the barbeque.

The simple steps:

- Fish in a parcel. Oil the shiny side of the foil. Wrap fish fillets in the foil to make a parcel. Make sure all parcels are similar in size and thickness. Add flavour and moisture to the parcels by adding herbs, spices, seasonings, aromatics (soy sauce, fish sauce, oyster sauce), vegetables, noodles, oil, or moisture in the form of wine, sake or beer. Ensure parcels are well closed before placing them on the grill. Don't overdo your additional ingredients, just choose three or four, one from each category, for example coriander, ginger, soy sauce, and sake.

- Fish fillet on the skin. Oil the grill before cooking. Season the fish and place skin side down onto the grill. Cover. Fish varieties that have a leathery skin are not suited.

- Fillet of fish directly on the medium hot grill. Oil the grill and cover. Turn fish with thin fish slice, possibly only two to three times, depending on the thickness of the fillet. Always remember to oil the grill first.

- Whole fish under 1 kg (sole, flounder, sardines, small trout) can be grilled directly on a medium hot grill. Again oil the grill and cover.

- Whole fish over 1 kg is best indirectly grilled with or without wrapping in foil. It is not necessary to turn the fish if you indirect grill. Cut to the bone at the thickest part of the fish to allow even heat penetration and flavours to permeate the fish.

The initiation test for the Gun Fish Grillers' Club is simple. You should be able to remove the top fillet off the whole fish easily when cooked, and then lift the whole bone structure and head in one piece off the bottom fillet. A complete fleshless skeleton and two perfectly cooked whole fillets of fish will proclaim you as one of the chosen few! Problems removing the top fillet will indicate the fish is undercooked. If the bone structure breaks up easily the fish is overcooked.

Meat & two veg!

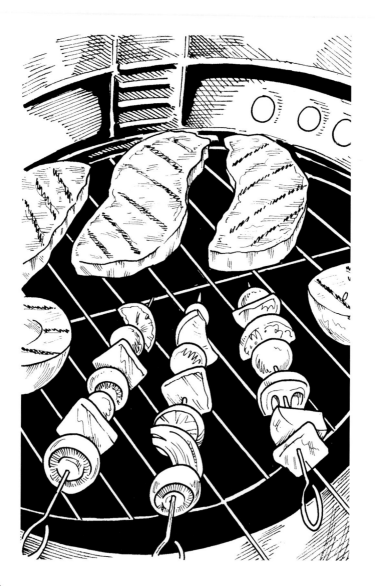

chapter 9
Meat & two veg!

You can't make a silk purse out of a sow's ear, and it
follows that however you cook some cuts, they will not
turn into juicy tender meat if you didn't start with quality.
Meat is the most expensive ingredient, so know what you
are paying for. Think less about the price while at the butcher
or supermarket, don't be too shy to ask about the quality
assurances and grading of the different meats. But just to
help you make a good choice, here's some simple advice:

Age
Connective tissue between muscles creates toughness.
The older the animal gets and the more the muscles are used,
the more connective tissues will be formed, thus younger
animals are more tender.

Sex
Male animals produce more testosterone as they get older
and taste different from females. A young goat is tender while
you wouldn't think of barbequing an old Billy.

Where does it come from?
As a general rule, those parts that had the most exercise are
the tougher cuts, while cuts along the middle back are more
tender, e.g. sirloin and tenderloin.

Breed

Different breeds give different quality and flavour of meat. Some breeds of sheep are specifically farmed for wool while others are bred and farmed specifically for meat.

Feed

"You are what you eat". The effect of the type and quantity of feed is quite clear. Grass-fed beef tastes different from grain-fed beef, and Scottish mutton raised on seaweed has a distinct and unique flavour. Japanese venerate Wagyu beef, grain-fed and heavily marbled with fat. (Incidentally, Wagyu is not ideal for barbequing because of the high fat).

Processing

Processing starts from the transport of the animals from the farm. Adrenaline, conditioning/ageing process, and packaging will affect the quality of the meat. The meat of top quality animals can be ruined by poor processing methods.

The cook

The last link in the chain. Good meat needs to be treated with respect and care. Select quality in the first place and cook it perfectly. Let all red meat rest after cooking/grilling and than carve it correctly – against the grain.

Vegetables, yes they too can be barbequed

Even if you are not a vegetarian, vegetables are a great food, and offer a huge variety of flavours, textures and colours to any meal. Don't be boring, give the old veg a go on the grill.

Vegetables suited to grilling:

- Bulbs   garlic, onion, leek.

- Roots   parsnip, carrots.

- Tubers   kumara (sweet potato), potatoes, yam.

- Stems and Shoots   asparagus, celery.

- Leaves   spinach, lettuce, Brussels sprouts.

- Flowers   broccoli, cauliflower.

- Vines   courgettes, squash, pumpkin, cucumber.

- Seeds and Pods   peas, beans, nuts.

- Fungi   mushrooms, truffles.

Vegetables for direct grilling:

Courgettes, eggplants, corn, asparagus, mushrooms, onion, peppers, tomatoes.

5–10 minutes on high heat. Brush with oil, season and grill.

Vegetables for indirect grilling:

Potatoes, kumara (sweet potato), yams, tomatoes, carrots, parsnips, swede, pumpkin.

Some of these vegetables can be hollowed out and stuffed with savoury filling. 35–45 minutes on 200°C/400°F.

Vegetables give you the opportunity to make excellent use of seasonings: dry and wet rubs, marinades, butters and sauces. Many can be stuffed, eggplant, courgette, tomato, are all delicious with cheesy or herb stuffings. And the humble veg can be a main course, a side dish or a condiment. A quick tip veggie extra: indirect grill a whole bulb of garlic. Don't do anything to it, just pop it on the barbeque for half an hour, until it feels soft. Then simply squeeze the bulb, the cooked garlic will come out the top of the bulb like toothpaste out of its tube. Spread it on steak, crusty bread or other veggies, or use as a dip. It doesn't get any easier, or tastier.

Getting fruity

For dessert or as accompaniments to meat, fruits of all kinds can be barbequed. A halved stoned peach with a sprinkling of icing sugar will grill quickly indirect. Once the sugar has caramelised the fruit is ready. Throw in peaches, nectarines, kiwifruit, apples and serve with pork loin. If you want a sweet treat, thick skinned fruits can be direct grilled and served with ice cream, or cream, hot off the grill.

Make a fruit kebab, or a grilled fruit salad – drizzle a little marsala over the hot fruit and toss it gently in a bowl. Kebabed large strawberries can be briefly grilled then given a sprinkle of lemon juice and a sifting of icing sugar. Bananas and pineapple are perfect, and a dash of rum will add a bit of warmth of another kind.

Kebabs, Kebobs, Satays, Sates ... food on a stick

Kebabs are an easy entrée or finger food offering or they can become the main course item of your grilling adventure. Kebab or kebob cooking is mainly associated with Middle Eastern dishes and metal skewers are used. Vegetables, chicken, beef, seafood or lamb are all suited to kebab cooking. Square skewers are easier to use than round.

Satay, or sate, originates from South East Asia. Bamboo skewers are used to hold the food while grilling on charcoal and the food is generally hotter and spicier than the Middle Eastern kebab.

Remember to soak bamboo skewers for half an hour before loading with tasty food. This prevents the stick from catching alight – an interesting trick at a circus, but not practical in domestic settings. Cut meat against the grain, and alternate ingredients on the skewer to give a colourful appearance. Don't pack them too tightly, and keep all pieces to an equal size to allow even cooking. Spare a thought for cooking times if a variety of ingredients are being used on one skewer – a mushroom will cook faster than a thick piece of meat, so consider thinly slicing the meat and threading it onto the skewer, or keeping the mushroom pressed well between the meat. Take care not to skewer yourself; a puncture from a blood soaked bamboo skewer can turn nasty. Buy good quality skewers – cheaper ones can split and be dangerous to eat from. Metal skewers are less exotic, but are reusable, safe and hygienic. Look for ones with insulated handles and a twist in the flat metal, to prevent food slipping off.

Good combinations for kebabs:

- Scallops, bacon and lemon.
- Pork, pineapple and green pepper.
- Ham, bananas and sweet potatoes.
- Steak, mushrooms and cherry tomatoes.
- Prawn, green pepper and pineapple.
- Turkey breast, nectarine and parsnip.
- Scallops, prawns and firm fish.

Spit roasting
& rotisserie

chapter 10
Spit roasting & rotisserie

Spit roasting

Spit roasting is the cooking of whole animals (lamb, pig, beef) or very large pieces of meat (saddle of beef) on a bar directly over or beside a wood fire (or better yet, the embers of a wood fire) or over gas, while rotating.

Rotisserie cooking is the same process but with smaller animals (chicken, rabbit) or pieces of meat (rib eye, loin of pork).

Some important aspects of spit roasting:

- Always centre the meat on the bar and secure well.

- Do not rotate meat directly over fire/embers, to avoid flare-ups.

- Adjust the distance to the fire (or shift the fire/embers) and the speed of rotation to regulate heat. The hotter the fire the faster the spit should rotate.

- It is better to cook longer with lower heat if the animal is large.

- Arrange extra heat by piling coals and embers near the thickest parts of the animal (shoulders, hindquarters).

- Use an instant-read thermometer or skewer in the thickest part to attest to doneness, juices should be clear.

The seven

deadly barbeque sins

- Start with meat that is totally thawed. If it's still slightly frozen in the middle, your meat will end up undercooked. Because of the low temperatures in the middle, your meat will look perfect on the outside and still be too raw inside.

- Try to avoid lighter fluid if you are cooking on a charcoal grill. The chemical flavour will really change the taste of your food.

- Cook at the right temperature. Hot and fast is not best for barbequing. To get the best smoke flavour and tender meat, it's best to cook long and slow. Except for steaks that need searing, medium heat is best.

- If you are using specialty wood, make sure it's aged. Using green wood will leave a bitter creosote coating on all your meat – very unappetizing!

- Put the lid down and leave it alone! A common sin is to keep lifting the lid to check the meat. Every time you open the lid, you drop the temperature in your grill. Relax. It's not going anywhere.

- If you use sauces or mops while your meat is on the grill, make sure it does not contain any sugar. Sugar burns at a low temperature and will burn onto the meat.

- The last barbeque sin is to use the same plate to carry the food back into the house. This is a food safety issue – nothing like food poisoning to ruin a party! Always use a clean plate.

On the spit

Nothing says caveman louder than a spit roast, when the meat is BIG and the fire is HOT. But, despite the apparent throwback to a time of greater simplicity, nothing is trickier than a spit roast. Originally it was the only way to cook a whole animal or large joint of meat. Pigs, lamb, saddle of beef, are all suitable for spit roasting. Some barbeques come with a rotisserie, or a rotisserie can be bought as an optional extra. A home made spit can be set up quite easily over a wood ember fire, provided you have the location and wind shelter.

The meat needs to be centred and well secured on the bar; uneven weight distribution will result in uneven cooking, and put a strain on the motor (or volunteer) turning the spit. The speed of the spit should be in accordance with the heat from the fire, low temperature = slow turning, high temperature = fast turning. If you are using charcoal or wood adjust the embers to be closer to the thicker parts of the animal (shoulders and hind legs) or further away (from the thinner parts) to alter temperature.

Larger animals and cuts should be cooked slower, which means on lower temperatures over a longer period. Keep the embers or heat source to the side of the meat, never directly underneath, as dripping fat will cause flare-ups that char the meat.

Keep yourself safe!

Spit roasting has significant dangers, the greatest being the potential for fat flare-ups. Pigs are particularly fatty, and an interesting experience taught me the lesson of fat flare-ups. At my wedding we had a suckling pig on a spit, rotating nicely as the guests mingled by the pool, in the hot New Zealand sunshine of a summer afternoon. Champagne, canapés ... flaming pig! Fat from our supper had turned the porker into an inferno, with squealing bridesmaids and alarmed new in-laws fleeing the scene. My best man and I (that's what best men are for) heaved the fiery pig into the pool, where it floated with a grin on its piggy face. Certainly a great way to make an impression, but I can assure you I prefer to make an impression today with a safe and productive spit roast.

Lesson learned: fatty food should never be roasted directly over the heat source! (Lesson Two: see my note on page 62 regarding trial runs before cooking for large numbers!).

Chicken on a stick

Many new barbeques come with a rotisserie accessory. An important thing to remember is that although these seem to be doing all the work for you, you should still observe the main safety rule of barbequing: don't leave the barbeque unattended.

That said, it is an easy way of getting your poultry evenly cooked — particularly larger birds. So here's how to put a bird on a rotisserie:

- Remove the neck.
- Clean and rinse the skin and cavity and pat dry.

- Remove excess fat at the cavity.
- Season the cavity.
- Fasten the neck skin to the back of the bird with a skewer.
- If you are using stuffing, insert it into the lower cavity then close the opening with skewers and lace up with butcher's string. The cavity doesn't need to be closed if no stuffing is used.
- Flatten the wings against the breast and secure with string.
- Tie the drumsticks to the tail.
- Slide one of the prongs on the bar with the points away from the handle.
- Push the rotisserie bar from the neck end through the bird till the prongs enter the bird fully.
- Slide the second set of prongs on the bar into the bird.
- Move the bird to the halfway point of the spit and fasten the prongs.
- Make sure the bird is properly balanced, adjust if necessary.
- Brush the bird with oil and season.
- Start spit roasting.

Chicken tip

Only season the skin of fowl if the skin is to be eaten. Your seasoning will not penetrate the skin and flavour your bird. Instead, rub your butter, seasonings or herbs under the skin then baste the skin with butter or oil before putting it on the grill or in your oven. This helps keep it moist and helps the browning process.

Lamb Argentinean style

I was a guest at a traditional Argentine barbeque and had the pleasure of enjoying a delicious slow cooked lamb. Similar to spit roasting, but with greater simplicity, the result was a unique flavoursome meal. This style of cooking requires quite a lot of space ... and meat eating neighbours – the apparently barbaric appearance could well upset any vegetarians living next door!

A circle of bricks or stones enclosed a large fire, with big logs burning all afternoon and evening. The whole lamb is spread-eagled on a kite-shaped cross, hindquarters uppermost. The cross is then stuck firmly in the ground at an angle so the meat is leaning over the embers of the fire. The meat is turned only once, and cooks very slowly. The only seasoning is salt.

Then, in Latino tradition, everyone plays football while waiting for the meat to be ready. When carved, the meat wasn't taken off the bone, but offered in enormous meaty chunks and chops that my Argentinean friends swear is the tastiest way to eat meat. Tasty indeed. A succulent, tender, smoky lamb, and an evening of fun and laughter, and, entirely coincidentally, quite a hangover the following day.

Grilling charts

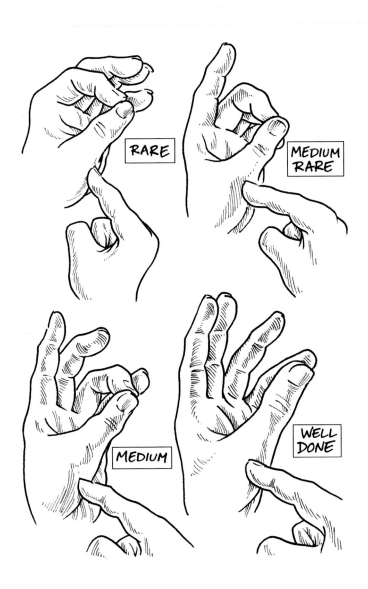

chapter 11
Grilling charts

I offer these grilling times with the proviso that in outdoor cooking other factors, mostly weather, can affect cooking times. If you use the times as a guideline, but employ the finger test for doneness of meats, and use an instant read thermometer for larger pieces of meat and poultry, then you should find this helpful.

Get a feel for the doneness of meat

Meat gets harder as the heat penetrates deeper into the centre so the obvious judgement is based on the softness or hardness of the meat. The softer the meat the more rare it is, and the firmer it feels the more well cooked the meat is.

The finger test:

Touch the top of each finger with your thumb. The muscle at the base of the thumb gets firmer as you move your thumb from the index finger to the next fingertip, until the little finger. Touch the meat with the index finger of the other hand and compare the feel with the feel of the muscle of the base of your thumb. Meat is rare when the thumb muscle is softest.

Rare   =   thumb to top of index finger.
Medium-rare   =   thumb to top of middle finger.
Medium   =   thumb to top of ring finger.
Well-done   =   thumb to little finger.

Checking fish for doneness

Use a knife or a fork to test the doneness of a fillet of fish.
The fish is done as soon as the meat starts to flake and the
fork or knife cuts easily through the meat. Don't overcook fish!
Gently flaking, moist flesh, but still delicate white colour, is
ready to eat, but greying, dry, firm flesh that is hard and breaks
rather than flakes is overcooked fish.

How cooked is that bird?

Use a knife with poultry and pork to check on the doneness.
Poultry should have clear juices and no pink should be seen
close to the bone. Slip a sharp knife into the thickest part of
the bird, and check the colour of juices that flow out. Pork
should be cooked but still juicy. A slight pinkness is acceptable,
but be wary you don't overcook. Hard and dry is no one's
preferred doneness!

Intensity of flavour of herbs and spices

Grading is from 1000 (strongest) till 0 (very little)

900	cayenne pepper	125	cardamom
800	mustard powder	115	tarragon
700	pickling spices	100	spearmint
600	cloves	95	rosemary
500	bay leaf	95	dill
475	ginger	90	oregano
450	black pepper	85	thyme
400	cinnamon	85	marjoram
390	white pepper	80	sage
380	star anise	75	parsley
360	nutmeg	70	sweet basil
340	mace	65	savory
320	caraway seed	65	aniseed
300	celery seed	60	chervil
290	cumin seed	60	onion
280	fennel seed	50	paprika
260	curry powder blend	40	saffron
250	allspice	25	sesame seed
240	mustard seed		
230	coriander seed		
220	turmeric		
150	peppermint		

Grilling charts

Use the grill charts as a guideline only. Before you begin cooking take note of the conditions (weather), barbeque, weight and thickness of larger pieces of meat, weight and thickness of whole fish, marinating times, and remember to record your results for future reference. Always rest red meat for a couple of minutes before cutting. 'Cooked' means completely cooked through.

BEEF			
Beef patty			
2cm (¾")	cooked	direct/medium	8–10 mins
Steak			
2.5cm (1")	med-rare	direct/high	4–5 min per side
Sirloin/rib eye/tenderloin/T-bone			
2–2.5cm (¾–1")	med-rare/med	direct/medium	5–7 min per side
2.5–5 cm (1–2")	rare/med	direct/medium	5–12 mins per side
Rib eye whole			
3.5kg (7.7lb)	med-rare	indirect/high	1¼ hrs
Eye fillet whole			
1.5kg (3.3lb)	med-rare	indirect/high	35 mins
LAMB			
Lamb patty			
2cm (¾")	cooked	direct/medium	
Lamb chop			
2–4cm (¾–1½")	med-rare/med	direct/medium	4–6 min per side
Rack of lamb			
450–700g (1lb–1½lb)	med-rare	indirect/high direct/medium	25 mins 25–35 mins

Boneless leg			
1–1½ kg (2–3½lb)	med-rare	indirect/high	35–45 mins

PORK

Steak chops			
2–2.5cm (¾–1")	cooked	direct/medium	10–15 mins
3–4cm (1¼–1½)	cooked	direct/high indirect/high	8 mins then 7–10 mins

Bratwurst			
	cooked	direct/medium	25–30 mins

Spare ribs			
1kg (2.2lb)	cooked	indirect/medium	2 hrs

Rib roast			
1–1½kg (2–3½lb)	cooked	indirect/medium	1½–2 hrs

VENISON

Steaks			
2cm (¾")	med-rare	direct/high	3 mins per side

Rack of venison			
700g (1½lb)	med-rare	indirect/high	35 min

POULTRY

Boneless breast			
125–155g (4–5oz)	cooked	direct/med	6–8 mins per side

Boneless thigh			
100–125g (3–4oz)	cooked	direct/med	6–8 mins per side

Chicken pieces, bone in			
	cooked	indirect/medium	40–45 mins

Whole chicken			
2kg (4½lb)	cooked	indirect/high	60–70 mins

Turkey			
	cooked	indirect/medium	2hrs per lb
Duck breast			
125g (4oz)	cooked	direct/medium	5–6 mins per side
SEAFOOD			
Fish fillet in parcel			
1cm (½")	cooked	direct/high	7 mins
On skin			
1–2cm (½–1")	cooked	indirect/high	11 mins
Fillet			
1–2cm (½–1")	cooked	direct/high	5–10 mins
Whole fish			
1–3kg (2.2–6.6lb)	cooked	indirect/high	20–60 mins
Lobster tail			
250g (½lb)	cooked	direct/high	8–10 mins per side
Scallops			
	cooked	direct/high	2–3 mins per side
Mussels			
Variety of sizes	cooked	steamed	8–12 mins
Shrimp			
Variety of sizes	cooked	direct/high	2–5 mins per side

The grilling times of whole fish depend more on the thickness than the weight. Use a medium heat when direct grilling pork and chicken.

VEGETABLES			
Asparagus		direct/medium	6–8 mins
Corn	husked	direct/medium	10–12 mins
	with husk	direct/medium	25–30 mins
Eggplant	½" slices	direct/medium	8–10 mins
Eggplant	halved	direct/medium	10–12 mins
Mushroom	Portabello	direct/medium	12–15 mins
Potatoes	whole	indirect/medium	45–60 min
Tomato	halved	direct/medium	6–8 mins
Zucchini	½" slices	direct/high	3–4 mins
	halved	direct/high	3–6 mins
FRUIT			
Apple	whole stuffed	indirect/medium	30–45 mins
Apricot	halved	direct/medium	6–8 mins
		indirect/high	8–10 mins
Bananas (ripe!)	whole skin on	direct/high	10–14 mins
Figs	whole stuffed	indirect/high	8–10 mins
Peach	halved	direct/medium	8–11 mins
		indirect/high	9–12 mins
Pear	wedges	direct/high	7–9 mins
	halved	direct/high	9–11 mins
Pineapple	skinned, cored rings	direct/high	4–8 mins
	skin on, cored, quartered	indirect/high	10–12 mins
Strawberries		direct/medium	4–5 mins

All normal people love meat. If I went to a barbeque and there was no meat, I would say "Yo Goober! Where's the meat!?" I'm trying to impress people here, Lisa. You don't win friends with salad.

Homer J Simpson

Raymond's favourite barbeque recipes

chapter 12
Raymond's favourite barbeque recipes

Over the years I have gathered, invented, adapted and adopted recipes from almost every possible source. Cookbooks, family, friends, even happy accidents can produce great tasting recipes. The internet is a possible source for recipe hunters, but be wary, there is no guarantee that the recipes will work or even be complete! If you find a good website, stick with it, and better yet, share it with your friends.

Family recipes are not only tried and true, but carry the memories of many happy occasions, serving up flavour and nostalgia. Experimentation—as I have said before, keep notes—can lead to some wonderful tasty innovations, but start with a 'safe' recipe form a good book, learn how to do it well, then try variations. You'll improve your cooking skills and maybe come up with a special signature dish of your very own.

I have below some of my favourites, and I am delighted to be able to share them with you. I cannot, however, lay claim to all of them, so thank here the many people and places that they have come from. To all the other fine BBQers, friends and strangers, thanks for your food!

Favourite Butters

Flavoured butters can be made on quiet afternoons and refrigerated or frozen. It is a good way of using up leftover fresh herbs or garlic that would otherwise be wasted. Room temperature butter is blended with the other ingredients and than rolled into a sausage in plastic wrap. Refrigerate or freeze at this stage. Cut slices about half a centimetre thick and place directly on the grilled food, or float a variety of butters in iced water, so the guests can choose their own.

> For all butters: 500g (1lb) of butter at room temperature mixed with the following ingredients:

Brown Butter

Ideal for grilled root vegetables especially sweet potatoes.

3 tablespoons muscovado sugar (or maple syrup)
1 teaspoon cinnamon
1 teaspoon grated orange rind
½ teaspoon cayenne pepper

Lime & Chilli Butter

This really is great with grilled corn or potatoes.

3 tablespoons lime juice
2 tablespoons chilli powder

Favourite recipes

Garlic Butter

Use with steaks, seafood, bread, or potatoes.

5 chopped cloves of garlic
2 teaspoons chopped parsley
½ teaspoon lemon or lime juice

Herb Butter

Combines well with vegetables and potatoes.

3 teaspoons chopped parsley
3 teaspoons chopped fresh French tarragon
2 teaspoons chopped spring onion or chives

Anchovies & Capers Butter

Especially lovely on seafood, chicken, vegetables, and bread.

5 chopped fillets of anchovies
5 chopped sun-dried tomatoes
3 teaspoons whole capers to be added after the ingredients
are blended with the butter.

Coriander Chilli Butter

250g (8oz) unsalted butter, softened
1 handful fresh coriander, chopped
1 fresh red chilli, seeded and chopped
1 tablespoon lime juice
2 teaspoons salt
1 teaspoon black pepper

Garlic Parsley Butter

250g (8oz) unsalted butter, softened
1 handful fresh coriander, chopped
5 garlic cloves, crushed
1 tablespoon lemon juice
2 teaspoons salt
1 teaspoon black pepper

Tarragon-Lemon Butter

Makes ½ cup – enough for 8 servings. Place these on steaks, chops especially veal and lamb, fish fillets or vegetables.

3 tablespoons finely chopped fresh tarragon leaves
1 clove garlic, minced
½ teaspoon finely grated lemon zest
8 tablespoons (1 stick) salted butter at room temperature
Freshly ground white or black peppercorn to taste

Blue Cheese Butter

Tasty with beef and vegetables.

2 tablespoons blue cheese
2 teaspoons chopped parsley
3 chopped cloves of garlic

Thai-Style Paste for Fish

This is a very simple way to add incredible flavour to fish.

2 lemongrass stalks	½ teaspoon ground cumin
2 tablespoons grated ginger	½ teaspoon paprika
5 garlic cloves, crushed	2 teaspoons salt
1 red onion, quartered	1 tablespoon sunflower oil
Grated zest of 1 lime	6 tablespoons dark sugar
2 teaspoons chilli flakes	6 tablespoons tomato puree
½ teaspoon ground coriander	

- Remove and discard tough outer skin of lemongrass stalks. Roughly chop. Put all ingredients into food processor and pulse until smooth. Coat fish evenly, cover and refrigerate for 2 hours before grilling.

- Paste can last a couple of weeks in the refrigerator as long as a film of oil covers it. As with curries, the taste of this paste only improves with age. You can fry it gently and stir it through rice for an extra zing in your accompaniment.

Chicken Satay

This is a variation of the satay my mother made; my Indonesian childhood was steeped in the flavours found in this recipe.

Serves 6

Marinade for satay:

1½kg (3.5lbs) chicken, beef, or pork meat
2 teaspoons ground turmeric
2 teaspoons ground coriander
2 teaspoons ground cumin
2 tablespoons sweet soy
2 cloves crushed garlic
Finely grated rind of ½ lemon
1½ teaspoons salt
1 tablespoon sugar

- Combine all the above in a bowl and stir to dissolve sugar.

- Marinate the meat for at least 1 hour and thread on soaked bamboo skewers.

- Grill over a high heat, preferably charcoal.

- Serve with spicy peanut sauce. You could try the making the sauce on the opposite page – it's delicious ... !

Spicy Peanut Sauce

This is my mother's recipe, she inspired me to cook – if I helped her in the kitchen I was allowed to have glass of beer!

2 medium onions, diced
4 chopped cloves of garlic
1 inch chopped fresh lemongrass or ½ teaspoon dried lemongrass powder
1½ teaspoons shrimp paste (belacan or trassi)
1½ teaspoons fresh chilli paste or finely chopped fresh chillies
3 tablespoons peanut or soya oil
2 cups peanut butter
Water
$^1/_3$ cup sweet soy sauce
$^1/_3$ cup coconut cream
Salt and pepper

- Mix onion, garlic, lemongrass, shrimp paste, and chillies, and make into a paste in mortar and pestle.

- Fry for about 3 minutes in hot oil and add peanut butter and soy sauce. Gradually add water till a thick sauce. Finish with coconut cream and seasoning.

- This sauce will last for a week in the refrigerator. Just add a little water when heating.

Tandoori Paste for Chops

Easier than the long list of ingredients would indicate!
For 20-25 chops you will need ...

1 quart, 950ml (2pts) of plain yoghurt
6 cloves garlic, coarsely chopped
2 inches fresh ginger, coarsely chopped
3 tablespoons cream
3 tablespoons fresh lemon juice
1½ teaspoons coarse salt
1 teaspoon ground coriander
½ teaspoon ground cumin
½ teaspoon ground turmeric
½ teaspoon ground black pepper
½ teaspoon cayenne pepper

- Make into a paste in blender.
- Marinate, covered in fridge, for at least 4 hours.
- Grill on medium high heat for 10-12 minutes.

Favourite Marinades

The simplest and tastiest of many recipes I've tried.

For pork & chicken:

½ cup sweet soy
3 tablespoons oil
½ teaspoon finely ground star anise
½ cup whole grain mustard
3 teaspoons Colman's dry mustard powder
½ cup sherry or sake
Salt and pepper

For beef:

2 crushed cloves of garlic
½ cup dark beer
2 tablespoons dark raw sugar
2 teaspoons Worcestershire sauce
1 tablespoon olive oil
2 teaspoons rock salt
1 teaspoon crushed black pepper

For meats, fish & poultry:

$2/3$ cup plain yoghurt
1 small onion, finely chopped
1 clove of garlic
1 teaspoon finely chopped/grated fresh ginger
1 teaspoon ground coriander seeds
1 teaspoon chopped Kaffir lime leaves
1 teaspoon ground cumin
½ teaspoon ground turmeric

BBQ Chicken Marinade

For 1 chicken or 8 chicken breasts (can also be used on pork).

3 tablespoons Hoi sin sauce
2 tablespoons apricot preserve or marmalade
1 tablespoon honey
1½ teaspoons fresh ginger chopped
1½ teaspoons oyster sauce
1½ teaspoons soy sauce
3 teaspoons Sake or sherry
1 teaspoon fresh chilli or chilli paste
¼ teaspoon Chinese Five Spice
1 teaspoon garlic finely chopped
½ teaspoon Kaffir lime leaves or lime rind, finely chopped

● Combine the ingredients in a bowl.

Wild Game Marinade with Juniper & Gin

For game, also pork, lamb or beef. Makes 4 cups, enough for 1.5kg (3lbs) of meat.

3 cups dry red wine
½ cup balsamic vinegar
½ cup extra virgin olive oil
2 tablespoons gin
1 medium onion, thinly sliced
1 stick celery, thinly sliced
2 cloves garlic, flattened
3 tablespoons chopped fresh parsley
2 teaspoons juniper berries
2 teaspoons black peppercorns
2 bay leaves
2 whole cloves
2 sprigs of fresh thyme, stripped
or ½ teaspoon dried thyme

- Combine the ingredients in a saucepan and bring to boil over medium high heat.

- Cool to room temperature.

- Use right away or transfer to a large jar, cover and refrigerate. The marinade will keep for several days.

Basic Barbeque Mop Sauce

2 cups distilled white vinegar
1 tablespoon coarse salt
1 teaspoon black pepper
1 teaspoon hot red pepper flakes
1 small onion, thinly sliced
1 jalapeno pepper, thinly sliced

- Place the vinegar, salt, black pepper and hot pepper flakes in a bowl and whisk until the salt dissolves.

- Stir in the onion and jalapeno. Taste for seasoning, adding black pepper or hot pepper flakes as necessary.

- Brush on grilled chicken or pork once the outside is cooked. The mop sauce can be made several hours in advance, but use it the same day.

Basic Bread Dough Recipe

Even my youngest child can make this bread easily; she makes the dough in the mixer with a hook attachment, but it's as simple to knead by hand.

2 tablespoons fresh baker's yeast
2 teaspoons sugar
2½ cups lukewarm water
6 cups plain flour
3–4 teaspoons salt to taste (or 2 tablespoons Italiano Rub)
5 tablespoons extra virgin olive oil

- Add sugar and salt to lukewarm water and sprinkle yeast over. Add flour and oil.

- Add seasonings such as fresh or dried herbs. Knead until smooth and elastic. Leave in a warm place to rise.

- Roll out to 2cm thick and place on oiled baking tray. Sprinkle with sea salt, herbs, or olives, brush with oil.

- Grill indirect for 35 minutes on hot barbeque.

Eggplant, Tomato and Feta Rolls

I've always been a meat eater, but this recipe opened my eyes, and taste buds, to the possibilities of vegetables. Tasty as either a side dish or a main.

2 large eggplants
Olive oil
10–12 sun-dried tomatoes
Handful chopped fresh basil leaves
5 oz Feta/Brie/Camembert cheese
Salt and pepper

- Slice eggplants lengthways into ½cm (¼") thick slices.
- Sprinkle with salt and allow to drain for 30 minutes.
- Rinse eggplant with cold water and dry well. Grill on hot grill for 6–7 minutes on medium high. Brush with a little oil while grilling.
- Arrange sun-dried tomatoes, basil, and cheese on the eggplant, and season.
- Roll and hold together with two toothpicks crossed.
- Keep warm before serving.

Grilled Salmon with Mustard, Horseradish, Rum & Capers

Easy and delicious! This never fails to impress guests, first with its appearance and then flavour. Serve hot with French bread.

Serves 6–8

1 side of salmon, skin on and boned
2 teaspoons capers
½ teaspoon coarse sea salt
1 tablespoon brown sugar (preferably Cane)

For paste:
2 tablespoons whole grain mustard
1 tablespoon mayonnaise
2 teaspoons good quality horseradish
2 tablespoons dark cane sugar (brown sugar is okay)
2 tablespoons dark rum
1 tablespoon fresh lemon juice
1 teaspoon of freshly ground black pepper
½ teaspoon of dried dill tops or 1 teaspoon of finely chopped fresh dill

- Combine all paste ingredients and spread generously over the flesh side of the salmon.

- Sprinkle capers, salt, and brown sugar over paste.

- Oil the grill and cook salmon, skin down, for 12–15 minutes using the indirect grill method with high heat.

- Serve immediately, don't chill.

Snapper Fillets with Chermoula

Snapper is a perfect fish for the barbeque (my favourite is Gurnard!), and this traditional North African paste is perfect with it. I usually serve it with grilled aubergine and tomatoes.

Serve 4

4 x 200g (7oz) fillets Snapper
200g (7oz) couscous
2 teaspoons chopped chargrilled pepper

For Charmoula paste:
3 garlic cloves
1 teaspoon salt
1 small onion diced
Small bunch of chopped fresh coriander
Small bunch of chopped fresh parsley
1 teaspoon paprika
½ teaspoon chilli powder
½ teaspoon cumin
6 tablespoons olive oil
Juice from 1 lemon

- Combine all ingredients and make into a paste using a food processor or mortar and pestle.
- Rub fillets in with paste and marinate for at least 20 minutes (keep 2 teaspoons paste aside for couscous).
- Grill on direct heat for approximately 9–10 minutes.
- Cook couscous and mix into it 2 teaspoons of paste and chargrilled pepper. Serve snapper on couscous.

Squid, Shrimps & Sweet Soy Salad

I am a big fan of Kaffir lime leaves; they boost flavour and add an exotic edge to every dish they are in.

For 4 entrée-size portions

3 medium size squid tubes cut in strips or rings
300g (10½oz) all purpose shrimps
200g (7oz) asparagus cleaned and cut in 1cm (½") lengths

For marinade:
2 chopped cloves garlic
2 chopped Kaffir lime leaves
1½ tablespoons sweet Thai chilli
3 tablespoons sweet soy
1 tablespoon chopped fresh coriander
Salt and pepper

- Combine all above ingredients and marinate squid, shrimps and asparagus for 30 minutes.

- Grill on very hot grill plate till squid changes colour (turns white).

- Serve on salad, garnished with lime wedges, strips of red pepper, and coriander leaves.

Beer Can Chicken with Cayenne & Cumin

Often dubbed my 'Drunken Chicken' this is a never fail, and the signature dish of my barbeque cooking courses; just remember to puncture the can!

Serves 4–6

A 2kg (4½lb) chicken
1 lukewarm can of beer

For the rub:
2 teaspoons paprika
2 teaspoons coarse sea salt
1 teaspoon freshly ground black pepper
1 teaspoon cayenne pepper
1 teaspoon cumin
1 teaspoon dried thyme

- Mix all ingredients and rub chicken from the outside, inside and in between the skin and breast meat.

- Open can of beer and empty (drink?) half of the contents.

- Pour a little of the rub in the can and insert the can into the cavity of the chicken. Spread the legs to use them as a tripod and place on a preheated hooded barbeque.

- Grill indirect for just over an hour on 190–200°C.

- Steamed beer keeps the chicken moist, and rub forms a spicy crispy skin.

Greek Garlic Chicken

Great for the middle of summer ... if you can't get to the Greek Isles at least enjoy some of the flavours in your own backyard.

Makes 4 servings
½ cup finely chopped fresh Italian parsley
¼ cup dry white wine
¼ cup extra virgin olive oil
2 tablespoons fresh lemon juice
1 tablespoon minced garlic
1 tablespoon black olive tapenade
1 teaspoon dried oregano
1 teaspoon paprika
½ teaspoon kosher salt
¼ teaspoon freshly ground black pepper

1 whole chicken, backbone and chest bone removed.

- In a medium bowl whisk together the marinade ingredients.

- Rinse the chicken pieces under cold water and pat dry with paper towels. Place in a large, re-sealable plastic bag and pour in the marinade. Press the air out of the bag and seal tightly. Turn the bag to distribute the marinade, place in a bowl and refrigerate for 4 to 6 hours, turning occasionally.

- Remove the chicken from the bag, reserving the marinade. Pour the marinade into a small saucepan, bring to the boil and boil for 1 minute. Set aside.

- Grill chicken indirect for about 80 minutes: 30 Minutes with meat side up and 50 minutes skin side up. Check if the juices run clear when separating leg from thigh.

Tequila Chicken Breasts

A friend of mine found this in an old magazine and has been mixing up Tequila cocktails and Tequila Chicken every summer since. Cheers mate, just remember to cook the chicken before you get into the Margaritas!

Makes 4 servings

For the marinade:
½ cup tightly packed fresh mint leaves
½ cup tightly packed fresh Italian parsley leaves
  with some stems
½ cup fresh orange juice
2 tablespoons tequila
2 tablespoons extra virgin olive oil
2 medium garlic cloves, crushed
2 teaspoons minced jalapeno pepper, without seeds
1½ teaspoons kosher salt
½ teaspoon ground cumin
½ teaspoon ground chilli powder
¼ teaspoon freshly ground black pepper

4 boneless chicken breast halves (with skin) about
170g (6oz) each.

● To make marinade: in a medium bowl whisk together the
  marinade ingredients.

- Rinse the chicken pieces under cold water and pat dry with paper towels. Place in a large, re-sealable plastic bag and pour in the marinade. Press the air out of the bag and seal tightly.

- Turn the bag to distribute the marinade, place in a bowl and refrigerate for 2 to 4 hours, turning occasionally.

- Remove the chicken from the bag, reserving the marinade. Pour the marinade into a small saucepan, bring to the boil and boil for 1 minute. Set aside.

- Grill the chicken breasts, skin side up, over direct medium heat until the meat is firm and the juices run clear, 8 to 12 minutes, turning and basting with the marinade once halfway through grilling time. Serve warm.

Moroccan Lamb Loin on Couscous

This is one of my own inventions. I love the warm spices with lamb, although it took a couple of attempts to get it just right. It takes a little bit of preparation, but it's well worth it.

Serves 4

4 lamb loins	For Moroccan rub:
½ medium onion finely chopped	½ teaspoon coriander seeds
3 cloves of garlic finely chopped	½ teaspoon cumin seeds
1 small tin peeled tomatoes	7 cardamom seeds
1 lime	1 cinnamon quill
½ cup lamb or beef stock	4 cloves
	½ cup paprika
	1 teaspoon garlic granulates
	Salt and pepper

To prepare rub:

- Toast coriander seeds, cumin seeds, cardamom, cinnamon cloves and ground. Add paprika, garlic salt and pepper. Rub the lamb with the rub and cover.

To prepare sauce:

- Sauté onion and garlic with 2 teaspoons rub. Add peeled tomatoes and stock. Simmer and add lime zest and juice of the lime.

- Rub the loin with spice mixture and grill lamb direct for 4 minutes on each side. Rest for two 2 minutes.

- Place on couscous and pour sauce over meat.

Grilled Salmon with Chilli & Kelp

4 portions of Salmon fillet on the skin (de-boned)
½ teaspoon chilli flakes
1 teaspoon dried kelp or wakame
2 teaspoons sea Lettuce (optional)
1 teaspoon finely ground dried Kaffir lime leaves
2 teaspoons Paprika
1½ teaspoons rock salt
1 teaspoon freshly ground black pepper
6 tablespoons extra virgin olive oil

- Mix all dry ingredients and add olive oil.

- Cover the salmon portions generously.

- On barbeque: oil grill and grill indirect (no heat directly under the portion and lid down) at 180–200°C/350–400°F for 15 minutes.

Grilled Butterflied Leg of Lamb with Mint Mustard

Mint and mustard seems an unusual mix, but the friend who dishes this up assured me it was good. It was.

Serves 6–8

¼ cup olive oil
3 cloves garlic, minced
Salt and freshly ground pepper
1 leg of lamb, 2–3kg (4½–6½lbs), trimmed of excess fat, boned and butterflied

For the mint mustard:
6 tablespoons chopped fresh mint, plus mint sprigs
   for garnish
3 tablespoons mayonnaise
¾ cup Dijon mustard
1 clove garlic, minced
1 teaspoon fresh lemon juice

- In a bowl, whisk together the olive oil, garlic, salt and pepper. Place the lamb in a shallow dish and rub the mixture over the entire surface of the meat. Cover and refrigerate overnight.

- To prepare the mint mustard, in a small bowl, stir together the chopped mint, mayonnaise, mustard, garlic and lemon juice. Set aside.

- Prepare a fire in a grill.

- Grill the lamb indirect for about 55 minutes on medium high.

- Transfer to a cutting board, cover loosely with aluminium foil, and let rest for 10 minutes before carving.

- Cut the lamb across the grain into thin slices and arrange on a warmed platter.

- Garnish with the mint sprigs and pass the mint mustard at the table. Serve immediately.

Smoked Fresh Ham

Serves 10 – 14

2 tablespoons coarse salt
2 teaspoons fresh ground pepper
2 teaspoons dried thyme
2 teaspoons dried sage
3 cloves garlic, minced
½ teaspoon ground allspice or cloves
1 shank-end partial leg of pork, about 5kg (11lbs),
    trimmed of excess fat and tied for roasting
2 tablespoons vegetable oil or olive oil

- Soak 3 handfuls of wood chips in water for about 1 hour.

- Prepare a fire for indirect-heat cooking in a covered grill.

- In a small bowl, stir together the salt, pepper, thyme, sage, garlic, and allspice or cloves. Pat the meat dry with paper towels.

- Rub the entire surface of the meat with the oil then rub the meat with the herb mixture.

- Scoop half of the soaked wood chips out of the water and drop them onto the fire. Place the pork on the centre of the grill rack, cover, and open the vents halfway. Cook for about 1 hour.

- Turn over the roast and add a few more coals to the fire if necessary to maintain a constant temperature. Scoop the remaining wood chips from the water and drop them onto the fire.

- Continue to cook until the pork is well browned all over and the herb rub has formed a dry, crispy crust, about 2 hours longer. Add coals as needed.

- Remove from the grill and transfer to a cutting board. Cover loosely with aluminium foil and let rest for 15 minutes.

- To serve, snip the strings, carve the meat across the grain into slices about 5mm (¼") thick, and arrange on a warm platter.

Grilles Peaches with Crème Fraiche, Amaretto & Pistachio Nuts

As we say in New Zealand, "Sweet as, mate!"

Serves 4

4 large, ripe peaches cut in half, stones removed
250g (8oz) crème fraiche
3 tablespoons pistachio nuts, chopped
2 tablespoons Amaretto
2 tablespoons dark cane sugar

- Mix crème fraiche, pistachio nuts and Amaretto and spoon the mixture into the peach halves.

- Sprinkle dark cane sugar over the filled peaches and grill (direct or indirect) on high heat for 12–13 minutes.

- Serve hot with a scoop of Cornish dairy ice-cream.

Grilled Pineapple with Cassia Bark, Star Anise, Cloves & Rum

Well worth tracking down the spices.

Serves 8

2 golden pineapples

Sauce ingredients:

2-inch cassia bark or cinnamon
2 star anise
5 cloves
$1/_3$ cup dark rum
250g (8oz) butter
250g (8oz) dark cane sugar

- Quarter the pineapple but keep leaves attached. Remove core and cut the pineapple meat off the skin. Cut in wedges and place back on the skin.

- Grind cassia, star anise and cloves and fry quickly in dry pan or wok.

- Melt butter and sugar on moderate heat while continuously stirring. Add spices and rum as soon as butter-sugar mixture has turned into a velvety sauce.

- Brush sauce in between the wedges and grill for about 10–12 minutes. Ensure leaves don't catch fire. Pour remaining sauce over the warmed pineapple just before serving.

Basics of Caramelised Dessert Sauces

All sorts of combinations are possible with the dessert sauces. The basic components are: butter, sugar and flavouring.

Never ever leave sugar cooking unattended. It will need constant stirring, and can boil very suddenly. Be warned, sugar sticks and burns more than boiling water, and so do take care of both your pots and yourself.

The general recipe is:

Melt equal amounts of butter and sugar in a pan over medium heat till the sugar is caramelised. It is important to stir during this process until all sugar is caramelised (sauce doesn't feel gritty).

- Then you can add flavouring such as spices and alcohol.
- Ideal spices for dessert: cinnamon, cassia bark, pimento or allspice, cloves, nutmeg, ginger, vanilla, star anise.
- Alcohol that could be used: rum, whisky, gin, vodka, tequila, Grand Marnier, Cointreau, cognac, Cocoribe, Galliano.
- Other flavourings could be: chocolate, coffee beans, maple syrup, orange rind, and lemon rind.
- Just keep experimenting till you create your own favourite recipe.

Useful checklists

GAS BARBEQUE BUYERS' CHECKLIST

What sort of barbequer are you? Patient and likely to cook 'American style' with hood down, even when direct grilling? Or are you more the impatient type: quick, high heat and direct grilling with hood up? If you belong to the 'patient' group you should be looking for brands produced for the US or Canadian market, (e.g. Weber Gas, Broilking, Brinkman, Titan etc).

The heat output of the elements needn't necessarily be high, but if you intend to direct grill with hood up and get that prime steak sizzling you will need to look for elements with high heat output (expressed in BTU or mega joule).

Brand

- Is the brand known?
- Is it supported by a good service and guarantees?
- Ensure there will be no problems obtaining spare parts.
- Are there other extras you can buy, specific to that barbeque?

Capacity

- Look for a hooded barbeque if you plan to barbeque more often and larger pieces of meat.
- Three gas burners are the minimum to grill indirect (with hood down).
- The more burners, the larger amount of food can be accommodated and the easier it is to control the temperatures under the hood (but the more gas is used!).

- Elements with a larger heat output will be needed if you tend to do more direct grilling (with the hood open or no hood).

- The heat output is less important if you grill with the hood down.

- Ventilation under the hood is important for efficient heat retention and control.

Flame tamers

- What sort? Metal, ceramic rocks, or lava rocks?

- Metal is easier to clean. Ceramic rocks and lava rocks need to be cleaned and replaced on a regular basis.

- The flame tamers shouldn't be too close to the grill surface, in order to avoid continuous flare-ups.

Thermostat

- A good working thermostat in the hood of a gas barbeque will assist you in maintaining the right temperatures.

Sturdy and safe?

- Does the unit feel sturdy when you shake the framework and the hood? Some models are top heavy and have a tendency to topple when rolled on uneven ground.

- Are the wheels well made and will they withstand constant moving to and from the garden shed?

Easy to clean?

- It is always hard to clean the barbeque after a good night of grilling. Stainless steel surfaces are easy maintenance. Enamel has a tendency to chip and rust after a while.
- Does the drip tray collect the fat and juices easily and is it removable to allow cleaning?

Gas knobs

- Are the knobs sturdy and don't come out easily? Gas igniters make the job easier.

Side burner

- A side burner is always handy to prepare sauces, stir-fry some vegetables or cook your potatoes.
- Will you be able to stay with the barbeque to prepare the meal?

Cover

- A cover gives the barbeque that extra protection when the barbeque is not in use.
- Make sure that any cover fits well, especially if the barbeque is to be stored outside where the wind could get underneath.
- A manufacturer's cover, made for your specific barbeque is always worth the extra cost.

CHARCOAL BARBEQUE BUYERS' CHECKLIST

Are you likely to grill the odd kebab, hamburger or small chicken fillet? Or do you intend to grill a large variety of meats, fish, poultry, vegetables, breads, pizza, etc.?

It isn't necessary to buy an expensive barbeque for charcoal barbequing. You can be very innovative in the creation of a vessel to hold the hot embers, charcoal or head beads/briquettes. A couple of bricks and a grill rack could be adequate to grill your satays perfectly. The Hibachi is such a simple vessel. It has a rack system to hold the grill at varying distances from the charcoal. However, if you barbeque a lot, and plan to cook large cuts of meat, a more sophisticated charcoal barbeque would be best.

What to look for:

- The grill surface should be a reasonable size and the bars of the grill surface should not be too thin.

- Think about the ease of cleaning when you are choosing the barbeque.

- A reasonable distance between the grill surface and the fire makes it possible to build uneven piles of charcoal or heat beads/briquettes to create different heat zones on the grilling surface.

- Ventilation holes under the heat grade helps to control and maintain the heat of the charcoal.

- A hood with ventilation holes is required for indirect grilling.

- The ball shape of the Weber Kettle, for instance, gives optimum heat rotation.

- The whole barbeque should be sturdy but easy to move and maintain.

- Badly made cheaper models rust away and often won't last for more than one season. Check the stability of legs, easy rotation of wheels and general quality of the construction material. A storing rack for the lid when it is off is useful.

- A thermostat in the hood is a nifty addition that makes it easier to maintain the correct heat.

- Look for a brand with a good distribution system and back up services such as guarantees and spare parts. If you use your barbeque frequently, you will eventually need replacement parts.

- Ask the salesperson if they have used the model you are interested in and what they thought of it. Ask specific questions. Of course they will want to sell it to you, but they should be able to answer very specific questions about its performance so keep 'grilling' them!

THE ULTIMATE BARBEQUE TOOL CHECKLIST

The tools you will need at your fingertips when you barbeque:

- Aluminium foil.
- Apron.
- Bamboo skewers.
- Basting brushes.
- Butcher's string.
- Chopping board.
- Cling wrap.
- Container for waste.
- Fish slice.
- Food tongs.
- Fuel – gas or charcoal.
- Jug for oil.
- Knives.
- Long barbeque tongs.
- Matches or gas lighter.
- Measuring spoons.
- Meat thermometer.
- Metal grill scraper.
- Metal skewers.
- Mortar and pestle or spice grinder.
- Oven glove(s).
- Serving spoons.
- Serving trays.
- Tea towels.
- Wok or saucepan.
- Wood chips.
- Wooden spoon.
- Zester.

BARBEQUE PARTY PLANNING CHECKLIST

For the perfect barbeque ensure that you have addressed all of the following:

Initial Questions

- What is the wet weather option?
- How many guests can I cope with?
- While I cook, how will they be entertained?
- Do I have space?
- Do I have the equipment?
- Any food restrictions (allergies, vegetarian etc)?

Menu Design Questions

- How much time will I have?
- Is food just part of the night, or a highlight?
- Who is able to help me?
- What is my budget?
- What food is in season?
- Do I want an easy going meal or to show off my skills?

Menu Details – Have I arranged...

- Shopping?
- Helping hands for the big night?
- Non-cooked dishes?
- Preparation of meats?
- Drinks preparation?

Time Plan

On the day/night have a pre-prepared schedule to work to.
If you change it, it doesn't matter, just having a rough guide will help you remember the most important steps.

- BBQ clean and safety check?
- Ingredients check – do I have everything?
- Fuel supply?
- Pre heat BBQs?
- Grilling times?
- Resting times?
- Last minute side dish preparations?
- Clearing and cleaning

Safety Checklist

- Clean barbeque
- Is it clear of windows, wooden fences, walls and overhanging branches?
- Is there a non-slip surface underfoot?
- Are pets and children clear?
- Fine salt (for oil/fat flares)
- Fire extinguisher
- Water (bucket or hose)
- Wind protection

THE BARBEQUER'S PANTRY BASICS

- Coarse salt
- Dark cane sugar
- Fine salt
- Fish sauce
- Horseradish
- Mustards
- Olive oil
- Pepper
- Sake
- Sesame oil
- Soy sauces
- Tabasco
- Vanilla pods
- Vinegar
- Wasabi (ground Japanese plant root)

Herbs & Spices

- All spice (pimento)
- Aniseed
- Basil
- Black pepper
- Cardamom
- Cassia black
- Cayenne pepper
- Chilli (flakes and ground)
- Chinese Five Spice
- Cinnamon (quills and ground)
- Cloves
- Coriander seeds
- Cumin
- Fennel seeds
- Garlic (granulated)
- Garlic powder
- Lemon pepper
- Mint (dried)
- Mustard seeds
- Mustard powder
- Nutmeg
- Onion powder or granules
- Oregano
- Paprika
- Parsley (dried)
- Rosemary
- Sage
- Sesame seeds
- Szechwan pepper
- Tarragon
- Thyme

Conversion
tables

Weight conversions

To convert ...	Multiply by ...
Grams to ounces	0.0353
Grams to pounds	0.0022
Kilograms to pounds	2.2046
Kilograms to tons	0.00098
Tonnes to tons	0.9842
Ounces to grams	28.35
Pounds to grams	453.592
Pounds to kilograms	0.4536
Tons to kilograms	1016.05
Tons to tonnes	1.016

Liquid conversions (approximate) – imperial, metric and US

Imperial	Metric	US Cups
½fl.oz	15ml	1 level tablespoon
1fl.oz	30ml	1/8 cup
2fl.oz	60ml	¼ cup
3fl.oz	90ml	3/8 cup
4fl.oz	125ml	½ cup
5fl.oz – ¼ pint	150ml	2/3 cup
6fl.oz	175ml	¾ cup
8fl.oz	250ml	1 cup
10fl.oz – ½ pint	300ml	1 ¼ cups

12fl.oz	375ml	1½ cups
1fl.oz	500ml	2 cups – 1 US pint
20fl.oz – 1 pint	600ml	2½ cups
1½ pints	900ml	3¾ cups
1¾ pints	1 litre	4 cups – 1 quart
2 pints	1¼ litres	1¼ quarts
2¹/₃ pints	1½ litres	3 US pints
3¼ pints	2 litres	2 quarts

Handy measures

The following are equivalent to approximately 1oz or 28g:

1 level tablespoon	Salt
3 level tablespoons	Flour
2 level tablespoons	Rice
5 level tablespoons	Grated cheese
4 level tablespoons	Cocoa powder
1 level tablespoon	Honey/syrup/jam
2 level tablespoons	Granulated sugar
3 level tablespoons	Sifted icing sugar
6 level tablespoons	Fresh breadcrumbs
4 level tablespoons	Porridge oats

Spoon measures

1 tablespoon (tblsp)	3 teaspoons
1 level tablespoon (tblsp)	15ml
1 level teaspoon (tsp)	5ml

- A tablespoon or tblsp., when referring to dry goods (i.e. flour etc.), usually means a rounded tablespoon.

- A rounded tablespoon means there is as much of the product you are measuring above the top edge of the spoon as there is in the 'bowl' of the spoon.

- A heaped tablespoon means as much as you can get onto the spoon without it falling off.

- A level tablespoon is where the ingredient is level only with the top edge of the spoon. To achieve this, fill the spoon and then run a knife horizontally across the top, discarding anything above the level of the spoon. Of course, do make sure you have something underneath to catch it!

- A stick of butter is equal to half a cup, 4oz, 8 tablespoons or 113g.

Index

'The Greatest Tips in the World' books

Baby & Toddler Tips
by Vicky Burford
ISBN 978-1-905151-70-7

Barbeque Tips
by Raymond van Rijk
ISBN 978-1-905151-68-4

Cat Tips by Joe Inglis
ISBN 978-1-905151-66-0

Cookery Tips
by Peter Osborne
ISBN 978-1-905151-64-6

Cricketing Tips
by R. Rotherham & G. Clifford
ISBN 978-1-905151-18-9

DIY Tips
by Chris Jones & Brian Lee
ISBN 978-1-905151-62-2

Dog Tips by Joe Inglis
ISBN 978-1-905151-67-7

Etiquette & Dining Tips
by Prof. R. Rotherham
ISBN 978-1-905151-21-9

Freelance Writing Tips
by Linda Jones
ISBN 978-1-905151-17-2

Gardening Tips
by Steve Brookes
ISBN 978-1-905151-60-8

Genealogy Tips
by M. Vincent-Northam
ISBN 978-1-905151-72-1

Golfing Tips
by John Cook
ISBN 978-1-905151-63-9

Horse & Pony Tips
by Joanne Bednall
ISBN 978-1-905151-19-6

Household Tips
by Vicky Burford
ISBN 978-1-905151-61-5

Personal Success Tips
by Brian Larcher
ISBN 978-1-905151-71-4

Podcasting Tips
by Malcolm Boyden
ISBN 978-1-905151-75-2

Property Developing Tips
by F. Morgan & P Morgan
ISBN 978-1-905151-69-1

Retirement Tips
by Tony Rossiter
ISBN 978-1-905151-28-8

Sex Tips
by Julie Peasgood
ISBN 978-1-905151-74-5

Travel Tips
by Simon Worsfold
ISBN 978-1-905151-73-8

Yoga Tips
by D. Gellineau & D. Robson
ISBN 978-1-905151-65-3

Pet Recipe books

The Greatest Feline Feasts in the World by Joe Inglis
ISBN 978-1-905151-50-9

The Greatest Doggie Dinners in the World by Joe Inglis
ISBN 978-1-905151-51-6

'The Greatest in the World' DVDs

The Greatest in the World – Gardening Tips
presented by Steve Brookes

The Greatest in the World – Yoga Tips
presented by David Gellineau and David Robson

The Greatest in the World – Cat & Kitten Tips
presented by Joe Inglis

The Greatest in the World – Dog & Puppy Tips
presented by Joe Inglis

For more information about currently available
and forthcoming book and DVD titles please visit:

www.thegreatestintheworld.com

or write to:

The Greatest in the World Ltd
PO Box 3182
Stratford-upon-Avon
Warwickshire CV37 7XW
United Kingdom

Tel / Fax: +44(0)1789 299616
Email: info@thegreatestintheworld.com

The author

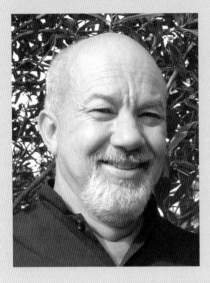

Indonesian born Dutchman Raymond van Rijk, now a New Zealand resident, runs 'Raymond's BBQ Gourmet' classes all over New Zealand and in Europe. Raymond's passion for food began in his mother's kitchen cooking Indonesian cuisine, and extended to encompass the breadth of European cuisine when he lived in Europe. He graduated from the School of Hotel Management, Maastricht, The Netherlands.

Seeking new horizons Raymond travelled to New Zealand in 1979 and settled there. His last twenty five years have been spent running a restaurant and catering operation in the wine country region of Hawke's Bay. Raymond now enjoys sharing his barbeque knowledge.

For more information please contact Raymond at BBQ Gourmet's website www.bbqgourmet.co.nz.